NATIONAL SECURITY MANAGEMENT

ELEMENTS OF DEFENSE ECONOMICS

Charles J. Hitch

and

Roland N. McKean

54200

INDUSTRIAL COLLEGE OF THE ARMED FORCES
WASHINGTON, D. C.
1967

INDUSTRIAL COLLEGE OF THE ARMED FORCES
WASHINGTON, D.C.

JOHN S. HARDY, Lieutenant General, USAF
Commandant

BRUCE E. KENDALL, Major General, USA
Deputy Commandant

RALPH F. LOCKE, Captain, USN
Director, Correspondence School

FOREWORD

The purpose of this text is to introduce the student to some of the essential elements of economic analysis which have come to play a vital part in Defense management since 1961. Much of this volume reflects research conducted by The RAND Corporation for the U.S. Air Force; and one of the principal authors, Charles J. Hitch, was to have the opportunity to put some of his ideas to the test in his role as Assistant Secretary of Defense (Comptroller) from 1961 to the summer of 1965.

Their work, the authors state, is not designed to solve military-economic problems at the various levels.

> ... We shall point out that certain policies stated in general terms, such as the protection of our deterrent forces, are extremely important, but we shall not, except in hypothetical examples, compare *specific* alternatives and indicate preferred strategies and weapon systems. This is the continuing task of responsible decision-makers and the analysts who advise and assist them. It can never be done once and for all because good solutions change with circumstances, and circumstances change constantly.

The authors' main purpose is "to help decision-makers, their advisers, and interested citizens in general, by showing how economic analysis—ranging from just straight thinking about alternative courses of action to systematic quantitative comparisons—can contribute to the selection of preferred (efficient, economical) policies and actions."

We introduce the student here only to portions of the authors' work. By way of essential background, we present in Part One the authors' view of economic factors that enter into the consideration of defense or national security problems (chapter I), and the kinds of threats that a nation's defenses are required to meet (chapter II).

Part Two is concerned with problems at a relatively high level—choices affecting the resources available for defense. Chapters III and IV are directly concerned with the determination of the defense budget—what the constraints are, and how we should choose the size of the budget.

Part Three is concerned with more specific problems—the problems of efficient choice within the departments responsible for defense—and with methods of analyzing various alternatives.

The authors' concern here is with "straight thinking" about military problems, especially the design of analyses and the use of appropriate economic criteria to aid in choosing preferred policies. In the four chapters comprising this part, the student is exposed to the complications associated with "incommensurables," uncertainty, the enemy, and time. Students with a strong interest in quantitative analysis and in some special problems and applications, looking at them as economic problems of choice, will want to consult the full work, *The Economics of Defense in the Nuclear Age*, from which this text is extracted, and the comprehensive bibliography acompanying that work. Students who need to reinforce and update their knowledge of general concepts of economics and of basic, college-level economics should consult one of the standard textbooks; some recognized writers on the subject are: Paul A. Samuelson, Melville J. Ulmer, George L. Bach, and Robert L. Heilbroner.

The College is indebted to The RAND Corporation for its permission to draw on the Hitch and McKean work for material to be used in orienting students in one of the basic disciplines of Defense management in today's environment.

CHARLES E. BARRETT
Professor of Economics

Industrial College of the Armed Forces
Washington, D.C.
5 May 1967

CONTENTS

ILLUSTRATIONS

PART ONE

ANALYTIC AND
FACTUAL BACKGROUND

I

DEFENSE AS AN ECONOMIC PROBLEM*

National security [1] depends upon many factors, which writers on the subject classify in different ways. Important among them are the morale of a country's soldiers, the number and ingenuity of its scientists, the character and skill of its political and military leaders, its geographic position relative to other countries, and even—in this nuclear age—the prevailing winds that blow across its expanses.

But national security also depends upon economic factors, which are variously interpreted and defined. Most speakers and writers who stress the importance of economic factors are referring to the economic strength of the nation, as contrasted with its military forces. They allege that the United States exerted a decisive influence in the later stages of World Wars I and II through its superior economic strength. Russia, it has been said, is more fearful of "Detroit" than of either the Strategic Air Command or the Divisions of NATO.

Other experts use the concept of economic factors more narrowly, to refer to the constraints on military forces imposed by the budget—the necessity to limit costs. Thus, Professor Kissinger [2] contrasts "doctrinal," "technological," and "fiscal" influences on our military strategy and concludes that the fiscal, as well as the technological, has been too influential at the expense of military

---

* The material which follows has been extracted from Charles J. Hitch and Roland N. McKean, *The Economics of Defense in the Nuclear Age* (Cambridge: Harvard University Press, 1960), with permission of the RAND Corporation.

[1] In most of this volume, the terms "defense" and "national security" will be used interchangeably. Wherever defense is used in a narrower sense, e.g., defense as opposed to offense, we believe the context will make this clear.

[2] Henry A. Kissinger, "Strategy and Organization," *Foreign Affairs*, April 1957, pp. 379–394.

doctrine. Similarly Mr. Hanson Baldwin complains that "In the Western World—though not in Russia—costs are a more decisive factor in shaping defense than is military logic." [3]

In this book we will be concerned with economics in its most general sense. Economics is not exclusively concerned, as the above interpretations imply, with certain types of activities (industrial) rather than others (military), or with the traditional points of view of budgeteers and comptrollers.[4] Being truly economical does not mean scrimping—reducing expenditures no matter how important the things to be bought. Nor does it mean implementing some stated doctrine regardless of cost. Rather economics is concerned with allocating resources—choosing doctrines and techniques—so as to get the most out of available resources. To economize in this sense may imply spending less on some things and more on others. But always economics or economizing means trying to make the most efficient use of the resources available in all activities in any circumstances.

In our view the problem of combining limited quantities of missiles, crews, bases, and maintenance facilities to "produce" a strategic air force that will maximize deterrence of enemy attack is just as much a problem in economics (although in some respects a harder one) as the problem of combining limited quantities of coke, iron ore, scrap, blast furnaces, and mill facilities to produce steel in such a way as to maximize profits. In both cases there is an objective, there are budgetary and other resource constraints, and there is a challenge to economize.

Economy and efficiency are two ways of looking at the same characteristic of an operation. If a manufacturer or a military commander has a fixed budget (or other fixed resources) and attempts to maximize his production or the attainment of his objective, we say that he has the problem of using his resources efficiently. But if his production goal or other objective is fixed, his problem is to economize on his use of resources, that is, to minimize his costs. These problems may sound like different problems; in fact they are logically equivalent. For any level of either budget or objective, the choices that maximize the attainment of an objective for a given budget are the same choices that minimize the cost of attaining that objective.[5] If the Bessemer process is the most economical method of producing steel from the one point of

---

[3] "Arms and the Atom—I," *New York Times*, May 14, 1957, p. 21.

[4] Problems of eliminating redundant overhead costs, preventing the padding of expense accounts, restricting the use of chauffeur-driven cars to top officials, etc., while important, are relatively narrow management problems, and not our concern in this book.

[5] This point is elaborated upon in Chapter V, below.

view, it is the most efficient from the other. If Missile X is the system that provides maximum deterrence with a $10 billion SAC budget, it is also the missile which most economically achieves that level of deterrence. In other words, there is no conflict of interest between the budgeteer who is supposed to be interested in economizing and the military commander who is supposed to be interested in efficiency—except in the determination of the *size* of the budget or the magnitude of the objective to be achieved. They should be able to agree on all the "subsequent" decisions.

For this reason it is misleading to imply, as do Kissinger and Baldwin in the articles just quoted, that economic or cost factors are necessarily in conflict with strategic, doctrinal, and technological considerations, and must somehow be reconciled with them, with not too much weight being assigned the economic. There *is* a conflict between defense and other goods in deciding on the size of the military budget.[6] Economizing involves deciding how much of other things to sacrifice in the interests of military strength. But in all decisions on how to spend the military budget —on what kinds of equipment and forces, to implement what kind of strategy—there is no such conflict. Strategy, technology, and economy are not three independent "considerations" to be assigned appropriate weights, but interdependent elements of the same problem. Strategies are *ways of using* budgets or resources to achieve military objectives. Technology defines the *possible* strategies. The economic problem is to choose that strategy, including equipment and everything else necessary to implement it, which is most efficient (maximizes the attainment of the objective with the given resources) or economical (minimizes the cost of achieving the given objective)—the strategy which is most efficient also being the most economical.

Strategy and cost are as interdependent as the front and rear sights of a rifle. One cannot assign relative weights to the importance of the positions of the front and rear sights. It does not make sense to ask the correct position of the rear sight except in relation to the front sight and the target. Similarly one cannot economize except in choosing strategies (or tactics or methods) to achieve objectives. The job of economizing, which some would delegate to budgeteers and comptrollers, cannot be distinguished from the whole task of making military decisions.

The problem of national security might in theory be regarded as one big economic problem. The nation has certain resources—now

---

[6] See Chapter IV, below.

and prospectively in the future—which are conventionally classified by economists as various sorts of land, labor, and capital. These resources can be used to satisfy many objectives of the nation and its individual citizens—national security, a high standard of living, social security, a rapid rate of economic growth, and so on. These are, of course, competing objectives. In general, the more resources the nation devotes to national security, the less it will have for social security and vice versa. We could (as some economists have done)[7] conceive of a "social welfare function" which we would attempt to maximize by an appropriate allocation of the nation's resources among the various activities satisfying these objectives.

In fact, for reasons which will become familiar as we proceed but are in any event obvious, this kind of approach to the problem of national security is completely impractical and sterile. We have to break economic problems, like so many others, into manageable pieces before we can make a good beginning at finding solutions. And in fact, in the United States and all other countries, governments and departments of defense are organized to deal with appropropriate parts of the grand problem at many different levels.

As a beginning let us consider economic problems at each of three rather gross levels. National security, from the point of view of an economist, may be said to depend on three things: (1) the quantity of national resources available, now and in the future; (2) the proportion of these resources allocated to national security purposes; and (3) the efficiency with which the resources so allocated are used.

Several parts of the government—including, for example, the Council of Economic Advisers and the Joint Congressional Committee on the Economic Report—are concerned with problems at the first and "highest" of these levels. Of course the quantity of resources existing in the present cannot be influenced by economic policy; but their full and productive employment can be, and so can their rate of growth, and therefore the quantity of resources that will be available in the future. Present resources are the consequence of past economic policies.

Problems at the second level are the special responsibility of the Bureau of the Budget and the Appropriations Committees of Congress, although all executive departments are deeply involved,

---

[7] See Kenneth J. Arrow, *Social Choice and Individual Values*, John Wiley and Sons, New York, 1951, and A. Bergson (Burk), "A Reformulation of Certain Aspects of Welfare Economics," *Quarterly Journal of Economics*, February 1938, pp. 310–334.

and every Congressman is interested. We decide the proportion of national resources to be devoted to defense when we vote a national security budget. In effect we are then choosing between more defense and more of other things. President Eisenhower has expressed this choice vividly:

> The cost of one modern heavy bomber is this: a modern brick school in more than 30 cities.
> It is two electric power plants, each serving a town of 60,000 population.
> It is two fine, fully equipped hospitals.
> It is some 50 miles of concrete highway.[8]

Problems at the third level—the efficient use of the resources allocated for defense—are primarily and in the first instance internal problems of the defense departments and agencies, although for reasons that we will have to examine, the President, other departments, and the Congress are concerned with the solutions to some of them. The problems consist in choosing efficiently, or economically, among the alternative methods of achieving military tasks or objectives. These alternative methods may be different strategies, different tactics, various forces, or different weapons.

It is not apparent to many who are unfamiliar with military problems how wide the range of choice really is. There is typically an infinity of ways to carry out a military mission, some much more efficient, or economical, than others. Consider the range of choice in the following three examples, taken from three different levels of decision-making within the departments of the government concerned with defense:

a. The provision of some measure of protection to the United States economy and population against atomic attack. The broad "pure" alternatives include: (1) widespread dispersal of industry and population before attack; (2) shelters and underground construction; (3) fighter and missile defenses; (4) full reliance on an atomic striking force for deterrence or in some circumstances, to destroy the enemy striking force on the ground. There are, of course, many ways of implementing each broad alternative, as well as many "mixes" or combinations of the pure alternatives.

b. Extension of the range of bomber aircraft. Broad alternatives include the use of: (1) operating bases farther forward, fixed or floating; (2) air refueling; (3) staging bases forward for ground refueling; (4) larger aircraft with greater fuel capacity. If there is time enough for a development program, additional alternatives would include the use of: (5) high energy fuels, chemical or

---

8 "The Chance for Peace," an address reprinted in *The Department of State Bulletin,* April 27, 1953, p. 600.

nuclear; (6) lighter structural materials; (7) boundary layer control; and many others.

c. The design of a new machine gun. There are many possible performance characteristics: range, accuracy, lethality of bullet, durability, reliability—some of which may have high military worth, some little. Each has its cost in money, development time, and production time; each its "trade-off" against other characteristics.

This factoring of the big economic problem into many subproblems at different levels has some disadvantages, which we will consider at appropriate places. But it makes both the analytical and the decision-making problems tractable, an advantage not to be lightly discarded. The sergeant in the *New Yorker* cartoon understands the point well when he shouts: "I'm telling you for the last time, Harwick. It's none of your business how much it costs the taxpayers. Your job is to fire that gun."

II

DEFENSE AGAINST WHAT?

During the last decade or so the development and accumulation of nuclear weapons—first by the United States, then by the USSR and finally by other nations—have revolutionized the problems of national security. No comparable technological revolution in weapons has ever before occurred in history. The analogy of gunpowder is frequently suggested, but the substitution of gunpowder took place gradually over a period of centuries; and, like the weapons it replaced, gunpowder was used almost exclusively in a circumscribed area known as the battlefield. Nuclear weapons, a few years after their invention, have made it feasible—indeed, cheap and easy—to destroy economies and populations. They will not necessarily be used for this purpose; but the fact that they can be so used profoundly influences the character of the security that is attainable, as well as the policies by which we must seek it. Today, or next year, or within ten years, any one of several nations can unilaterally destroy the major cities of the others, and the latter, if they are prepared and respond quickly, can make the destruction mutual. In these circumstances, problems which once dominated our thinking about defense become unimportant. And while other problems assume new importance, we have scarcely had time to learn what they are, let alone how to think about them.

Because the weapons environment critically influences choice of policy, this chapter will first describe and project the weapon developments themselves, and then attempt to trace their implications for the kinds of war that our policies should be designed to prepare for or prevent. At this point we shall be concerned with the technological possibilities in the absence of any agreement to disarm or adopt significant limitations on the use of weapons.

WEAPON DEVELOPMENTS

Enough is known concerning the development and production of nuclear weapons and the means of delivering them—both here and in the USSR—for a general consideration of medium- and long-term policies. For this purpose we can collapse the next decade or so to the present point in time. Exact estimates of present or near-future capabilities of both the United States and the USSR in terms of thermonuclear weapons and carriers are not here required. The significant facts are plain enough to informed public opinion throughout the world. They may be summarized as follows:

1. The number of urban centers which account for most of the economic strength of a major military power like the United States or Russia is small—certainly not more than a few hundred. Fifty-four United States metropolitan areas contain sixty per cent of the nation's manufacturing industry. Their population of well over 65,000,000, while only forty per cent of the national total, includes a much larger proportion of the nation's highly skilled technical, scientific, and managerial personnel. The 170 metropolitan areas listed by the Census Bureau contain seventy-five per cent of manufacturing industry and fifty-five per cent of the nation's population.[1] The concentration of industry in Russian urban centers appears to be roughly the same as in the United States, although the centers themselves tend to be more compact and therefore easier targets. While the total Russian population is less concentrated than that of the United States (almost half live on farms), the concentration of industrial and skilled labor and management is at least as great. Britain, Germany, and other industrial countries present even fewer targets.

The elimination of fewer than 200 metropolitan areas in either the United States or the USSR (still fewer elsewhere) would therefore, as a direct effect, reduce industrial capital by 75 per cent and the most valuable human resources by about as much. This, in itself, would demote a first-class power to third class, but to the direct effects must be added indirect ones. Because of the interdependence in a modern industrial economy, the productivity of the surviving unbalanced economic resources would be reduced, perhaps disastrously. Radioactive fallout would be likely to inflict serious casualties on populations outside the target cities.

2. How many bombs would be required to "eliminate" a metropolitan area? It depends, of course, upon the size and shape of the area and the size of the bomb as well as upon other factors. But we were told by the Chairman of the Atomic Energy Commission

---

[1] The metropolitan area concept as defined by the Census Bureau is, unfortunately, not a perfectly satisfactory measure of urbanization—because its definition is primarily on a county unit basis. The figures above include, therefore, some capital and population which may be sufficiently far from presumed city targets as not to be vulnerable to the direct effects of urban bombing, except fallout. On the other hand, the arbitrary legal boundaries of cities are much too restricted and even less satisfactory for our purposes.

after one test in the Pacific that a thermonuclear explosion could destroy any city on earth.[2] We know that very much smaller bombs will destroy small cities, as the first primitive 20 kiloton atomic bomb destroyed Hiroshima, a city of 250,000, killing a third of its population; that thermonuclear weapons have been made in the multi-megaton "yield" range; and that the area of destruction from blast increases as the two-thirds power of the yield (thus, a ten megaton bomb would devastate an area approximately sixty times as great as that devastated by a twenty kiloton bomb). We have also been told that the area of intense radioactive fallout from the Bikini shot was 7,000 square miles—that is, an area fifteen times the size of Los Angeles or approximately equal to the total land area of New Jersey.

About the long-term radiation hazards from such fission products as strontium-90 and cesium-137 we know less. The dangers resulting from a large-scale attack would be significant, though they may not affect the number of weapons that "rational" attackers would be willing to dispatch.

In any event, we are clearly entering a one-bomb-to-one-large-city era, which means usually one, perhaps occasionally two or three, bombs per metropolitan area. Barring large-scale passive defenses, total bomb-on-target requirements to destroy urban concentrations in the United States appear to be in the low hundreds, even allowing some to be assigned to economic targets outside cities. A larger number of bombs would have to be dispatched if delivered by missiles with low accuracy or reliability. Against a very effective air defense the number dispatched might have to be several times the number required on target—but we are told that no completely effective air defense is in existence and, as we shall see, it is questionable how effective air defense can be made against surprise attack.

3. Nuclear weapons of the same kind or in their small, light, "tactical" guise [3] may revolutionize war on the ground and at sea as drastically as the strategic air war. Less is evident about "requirements" for nuclear weapons against military targets: the number needed to destroy some highly dispersed and "hardened" military forces could be very large. What is evident is (1) that tactical forces armed with even moderate numbers of nuclear weapons and the means of delivering them can easily and quickly

---

[2] *New York Times*, April 1, 1954. Mr. Strauss was not using "destroy" in a literal physical sense, and he was undoubtedly implicitly assuming no large-scale expensive passive defense measures to reduce vulnerability.

[3] The largest "strategic" thermonuclear weapons may be even more effective against some military targets, e.g., by making huge areas uninhabitable for long periods.

defeat forces which do not possess them; (2) that both the United States and Russia can use such weapons, and (3) that ground, naval, or tactical air forces that have not adapted their deployment and tactics to the new weapons will be hopelessly vulnerable to nuclear attack.

4. While Russia's weapon technology and nuclear stockpile *may* still lag behind ours, it would be rash indeed to expect any such lags to widen. As to technology, the Russians have obviously made tremendous progress in rocket engines and missiles, and quite possibly have more first-rate scientists working on their programs than the United States has in its programs. As to nuclear stockpiles, increases in production rates on both sides depend mainly on a willingness to invest in additional productive capacity. No one believes any longer that a shortage of some crucial specific resource like uranium ore will conveniently (for us) inhibit Soviet production. The Soviet Union is compelled by the strongest of motives to match or surpass the United States programs, and has not hesitated in the past to undertake very large investment programs (for example, in steel) to meet security objectives.

Several implications of these weapon developments for the relative strengths of offense and defense have become fairly clear. These implications may be summarized in the following way.

1. The game is loaded against the defense when small-scale (by World War II standards) sudden attacks can cause catastrophic and perhaps irreparable damage.

2. Responsible officials of the Air Force and of the North American Air Defense Command have told us repeatedly that a leak-proof defense is not now attainable. Under some, not too unlikely, circumstances of surprise attack, we could fare very badly.[4]

While air defenses can undoubtedly be vastly improved over the next few years, the offense is likely to improve concomitantly. Ballistic missiles present formidable problems for air defense.

3. The superiority of the offense does not necessarily imply that either side can eliminate the enemy's ability to retaliate in force; still less that either side can *guarantee* such elimination. A strategic bombing force is much easier to protect by active and passive measures and by mobility and concealment than are economic and population targets. Such developments as nuclear-powered submarines armed with Polaris and train-mobile Minuteman missiles are offensive weapons with revolutionary implications.

---

[4] We could of course do much better against a *small* attacking force *if we had adequate warning* than we could in less favorable circumstances.

Moreover, the development of thermonuclear weapons, by greatly reducing the number of bombs on target required to cause massive damage to economic and population targets, has enhanced the retaliatory capability of whatever portion of one's striking force manages to escape surprise enemy attack. Unless the attacker is extremely successful, he may fail to prevent effective retaliation.

4. Similar considerations apply to tactical engagements, on the ground and at sea. Nuclear weapons and modern delivery systems give an attacker the ability to compress a devastating attack in space and time. Again we appear to have made much greater progress in offensive missiles than in missile defenses. And here, as in the strategic war, it is hard for the attacker to insure against effective counterattack.

That the superiority of the offense will persist is, of course, not certain. Judgments about the future rarely are. The revolution in military technology which began with the atomic bomb is a continuing, even perhaps an accelerating, one and will certainly take unexpected, unpredictable turns. And the fact that the odds favor the offense by no means implies that attempts to provide any defense are a foolish waste of resources. On the contrary, some kinds of defense measures are essential and integral components of a strategy of deterrence. But the prospects are poor that we will ever again be able to rely on such defenses to prevent great destruction if deterrence fails and an attack is launched.

IMPLICATIONS FOR KIND OF WAR

The weapon developments that have been described could conceivably influence the character of warfare in either of two directions, neither of which can be ignored in our plans. They could increase the violence of war, or they could limit it.

All-Out Thermonuclear War and Limited Local Conflicts

Most obviously, these developments could make war "total" to a degree never before experienced. An all-out thermonuclear war involving nations like the United States and the Soviet Union could easily destroy either or both, at least as powers of any consequence, in a matter of days or perhaps even hours.

There is increasing recognition, however, that the dangers implicit in participation in all-out thermonuclear war may result in a stalemate. In the words of Sir Winston Churchill, a "balance of terror" may replace the balance of power. Nations may become too fearful and cautious to use or even threaten to use their ultimate weapons, except for direct self-protection. This would mean, assuming no change in the objectives of Russia or Red China, a continuation of the cold war, with the Russians and Chinese attempting to win uncommitted areas by political and economic warfare, by subversion, and by limited, local military aggression. To avoid piecemeal surrender, we might determine to engage in defensive or counter-military actions also limited in character.[5]

These military actions, or limited, local wars, may flare up as a result—indeed as an extension—of international negotiation, of internal revolution, or of pawn moves by major powers to test or exploit a weakness. They are the late twentieth century "balance of terror" counterpart of the limited-scale, limited-objectives wars of the "balance of power" century between Waterloo and World War I. We have seen many of these limited wars in recent years: the contest in the Formosa Straits, the Indo-China War, the Korean War (small only in comparison with World War II), the Greek-Albanian-Yugoslav conflicts, the Chinese Civil War, the Indonesian revolutions, the Suez invasion, the Lebanon crisis, and others. While some of these were not of primary concern to the major powers, most of them were. Challenges (or opportunities) like Greece, Korea, and Suez will continue to present themselves.

The recent history of restraint in the use of nuclear weapons,[6] of attempts to confine these conflicts, of negotiated armistices, of ability to swallow frustration where the outcome was completely adverse (as for us in Indo-China and for the USSR in Greece)— all these are significant indications that the war of limited scale and limited objectives is here to stay.

But so is the danger of thermonuclear war, despite its recognized suicidal threat. There are many ways in which all-out war could be triggered by accident or misunderstanding. Either side may resort to a thermonuclear strike to protect some presumed vital interest (for example, on our side, Western Europe), or in frustration or desperation (for example, if the cold war appears to be going hopelessly against it), gambling upon the very great advantages accruing from a surprise first strike. Finally, the very fearsomeness of the threat is an invitation to a calculating, ruthless power to remove it by force if any happy circumstance presents itself—as, for example, the temporary impotence or vulnerability of the opposing strategic air force; or his own temporary

---

[5] See Henry A. Kissinger, *Nuclear Weapons and Foreign Policy*, Harper and Bros., New York 1957, Chapter 5 and *passim*, for an extreme but persuasive statement of this argument.

[6] We would by no means rule out the use of tactical atomic weapons in local wars; in fact, there have been numerous authoritative statements that the U.S. will so use them. But past restraint must be explained in part by the fear that their use would make it more difficult to limit the scale and objectives of the conflict.

invulnerability resulting from, say, a breakthrough in air defense technology. Moreover, in considering the prospects of some power initiating thermonuclear war, we cannot confine ourselves to the Soviet Union and the United States. Within the next ten to twenty years (not too long a period for the weighing of some military economic policies) several nations in addition to the United States and the USSR are likely to acquire a substantial thermonuclear capability. Quite apart from specifically military atomic programs, the widespread use of reactors for power will result in stocks of nuclear materials that may find their way into weapons.

It appears then that in our national security planning we must consider at least two kinds of war—all-out thermonuclear war on the one hand, and limited, local actions of a holding or counter-offensive character on the other.

The relative probabilities of these two kinds of war occurring will depend in part on the policies we pursue. If we prepare to deal with only one, we invite defeat, indeed destruction, by the other. The number of kinds of war which we must consider cannot, therefore, be reduced below two.

War Calling for Prolonged Mobilization

Does the number have to be increased to three? Is there a third kind of war, besides total and local wars, for which we must prepare? It has sometimes been suggested that a third possibility is a large-scale and long war, like World War II, in which strategic bombing of cities is either withheld or, if attempted, is ineffective *on both sides*.[7] Let us call this the World War II type war, although it might differ from World War II in such important military aspects as the widespread use of atomic weapons against military targets.

The question whether this World War II type of war is likely enough or dangerous enough to justify extensive preparations is, as will be seen, a crucial one for economic mobilization policy. We will simply state our views, because to defend them would carry the discussion far beyond its intended scope.

The contingency that strategic bombing would be attempted but ineffective *on both sides* seems to be extremely unlikely, for reasons already explained.

Mutual withholding of strategic attacks on cities for fear of retaliation is a somewhat more serious possibility—but only if the withholding is combined with quite limited war objectives: If the apparent winner presses on for anything like "unconditional sur-

---

[7] If ineffective on only one side, the strategic bombing would be decisive and the war short.

render," the apparent loser would convert the limited war to a total one. But a limited objectives war would be unlikely to be large-scale and long, like World War II. Mutual withholding plus limited objectives define what is essentially a local action.[8]

If a war of this kind did occur, we would have time to mobilize our industrial potential and ought to "win" eventually, just as we did in World War I and World War II, even if we were relatively unprepared at its beginning.[9]

In short, this kind of war appears to be the least likely (of the three) and least important in our preparations. It might become most important if atomic disarmament is achieved. But this has not looked very promising, and effectively controlled atomic disarmament (the only kind that United States policy has contemplated) may no longer be feasible unless completely new ideas for inspection and enforcement are conceived and accepted.[10]

Some British writers have suggested that the contestants might fight a lengthy "broken-back war" to a conclusion on the ground *after* successful strategic bombing on both sides. This would be Phase II of an all-out thermonuclear war. We should not completely ignore it in our planning, yet it is obviously not too important if Phase I is completely successful on both sides, or if one side falls substantially shorter of complete success than the other.

IMPLICATIONS FOR THE IMPORTANCE OF ECONOMIC STRENGTH

Declining Importance of Economic War Potential in Its Conventional Sense

The term "economic war potential" has usually meant the maximum *fully mobilized* capability of an economy to supply the men and materials required to fight a war. There are two objections to this concept. The first is its vagueness. What constitutes a "maximum" diversion of resources to war depends importantly upon (a) political and morale factors which in all countries fluctuate with circumstances, and (b) the time allowed for conversion to war production: the longer the mobilization period, the greater the peak war output. There is no single number or simple set of

---

[8] There are other difficulties associated with mutual withholding of city bombing in any war transcending a local action. There may be no practicable way to delimit the restriction: we know that many "strictly military" targets are separated from large centers of population by less than the lethal radius of large bombs.

[9] This is almost a *reductio ad absurdum*. Russia would not allow us to win complete victory while she possessed a nuclear stockpile.

[10] See Eugene Rabinowitch, "Living with H-Bombs," *Bulletin of the Atomic Scientists*, Vol. XI, No. 1, January 1955, pp. 5–8.

numbers which can respect "the" economic war potential of a nation.

Second, and more important, recent and prospective technological developments associated with nuclear weapons have greatly reduced the significance of economic war potential in the sense of maximum fully mobilized capacity for war production. Before the development of nuclear weapons and the means of delivering them on distant targets, the military power of the United States could be fairly well measured by its economic potential. Geography afforded us the time we needed, if pressed, to translate most of our potential into power.[11] Because we were the wealthiest nation in the world with the largest steel and machinery industries, we were also the most powerful militarily.

The development of nuclear and especially of thermonuclear weapons represents a momentous turning point in the cost of acquiring military capabilities. Destructive power has now become so cheap that wars can be won or economies destroyed before there is time for mobilization.

In an all-out thermonuclear war the superior economic war potential of the United States is important only to the extent that it has been effectively diverted to security purposes before war starts. This is true for all our forces, offensive or defensive. It is particularly and most obviously true for our strategic air offensive forces and air defense. For preparedness for full thermonuclear war the United States must learn to rely on forces in being—not as cadres about which much larger, newly mobilized forces will be organized, but as *the* important forces.

Economic war potential also appears to be less than decisive in fighting local wars (Viet Minh could defeat France in the jungles of Northern Indo-China), and of even less importance, as potential, in countering assaults by infiltration, subversion, civil war, and astute diplomacy. In limited wars, too, forces in being seem likely to play a crucial role, useful reserves being mainly those that can be mobilized promptly. Once hostilities have begun, industrial potential cannot be brought to bear soon enough. Even in World War II, the industrial potential of the allies did not save France or count for much in the first two or three years.[12] More recently, in the Korean War, industrial potential was not the force that saved the port of Pusan or shaped the course of the conflict. In all such action—limited in objectives, means, and scope—full indus-

---

[11] Even before the development of nuclear weapons, geography proved an inadequate defense for European countries against Blitzkrieg tactics based on aircraft and tanks.

[12] See C. J. Hitch, *America's Economic Strength*, Oxford University Press, London, 1941, pp. 60–73, 95–110.

trial mobilization is not approached, and economic war potential never comes into play.

In consequence the significance of economic war potential in its usual meaning has been degraded. The nation which can maintain the most formidable forces in being is not necessarily the wealthiest. In peacetime the proportion of national resources that can be diverted to national security purposes is by no means constant among nations. Both in peacetime and in fighting limited wars, countries with less economic war *potential* may support larger military budgets and forces. Russia, for example, a much poorer country than the United States, has supported a larger peacetime military program.

This situation is a particularly dangerous one for the United States. Shielded by geography, we have traditionally (before the Korean War) maintained very small forces in peacetime, and have regarded them as cadres rather than as integrated fighting units in a state of readiness. There is a strong tendency for nations (like individuals) to persist in policies which have been successful long after the external conditions essential to success have vanished, especially when they are pleasant and cheap like this one. The United States will probably maintain a substantial industrial lead over possible enemies for many years, but if we rely upon it as mobilization potential as we did before World War II, we will be inviting irrevocable disaster.

The Importance of Economic Strength Before the Outbreak of War

Without doubt, then, "the nostalgic idea that our industrial power is our greatest military asset could ruin our military planning." [13] This does not mean, however, that economic strength will be any less important in the pursuit of national objectives in the future than in the past. Military power is derived from economic strength, and foreign policy is based on both. Economic strength that is used for national security purposes *in time* is the embodiment of military power. Using it in time demands a new approach to national security problems—which to some extent we have already made.

The essential contribution of economic strength is that it enables us to do more of the numerous things which are desirable from the point of view of national security, but which, in their fullness, not even the wealthiest nation can afford.

---

[13] Thomas K. Finletter, *Power and Policy*, Harcourt, Brace and Company, New York, 1954, p. 256.

What are these desirable things in a thermonuclear era—that is, things that have positive payoffs and that we would like to have if resources were unlimited?

1. Preparations for and deterrence of thermonuclear war. These would include strategic air forces, warning networks, active air defenses, and passive defenses of various kinds including perhaps dispersal, shelters, and large-scale stockpiling of both weapons and industrial commodities. It appears desirable not only to do all these things but to do them in style—to confront the Soviet Union with a variety of strategic air threats, each absolutely invulnerable to any conceivable weapon which might be used against it; to erect a continental air defense system embodying all the latest and most expensive equipment of which any scientist has dreamed; and to buy enough passive defense of all kinds to insure our survival if by any chance an enemy attack still gets through.

2. Preparations for local and limited wars also appear desirable: challenges to fight such wars are almost certain to occur, and it would be comforting to be able to accept such challenges, or to make counterchallenges, if we want to. Sometimes it is argued that limited wars can be handled without ground forces or tactical air power simply by threatening massive retaliation against any and all provocations. If this were true, conventional military forces would be superfluous. The trouble is that the enemy might not believe our threat to launch a thermonuclear attack in the event of minor provocations.[14] Moreover, he might be correct in disbelieving, for we are probably not willing to use H-bombs to cope with minor aggressions—partly to avoid inhumane destruction, partly to retain allies, but mostly to escape the H-bombs that could in turn descend on us. Consequently, without conventional forces, we might have nothing with which to counter local aggressions and be wide open to "nibbling" tactics by the enemy. The net result might also be a heightened probability of thermonuclear war.

Preparation in style also seems desirable. Local, limited wars have taken many forms and have occurred in many places in recent history; future possibilities are even more numerous. We might have to fight in Southeast Asia, the Middle East, or the Balkans, with or without atomic bombs, with native help of varying qualities. We should like to have heavy matériel stocks pre-

---

14 For a discussion of these issues, see Bernard Brodie, "Unlimited Weapons and Limited War," *The Reporter*, November 18, 1954, pp. 16–21; and William Kaufmann, "Limited Warfare," in W. Kaufmann (ed.), *Military Policy and National Security*, Princeton University Press, Princeton, N.J., 1956, pp. 102–36.

positioned and, in addition, a large capacity for moving men and matériel rapidly by sea and by air to the theater of action. To back up our ready forces for such wars it would be desirable to have trained reserves and facilities for quickly expanding the production of matériel.

3. It would be desirable too (if resources were unlimited) to prepare to fight a World War II type of war. Even though this sort of conflict seems unlikely, it might conceivably occur. Preparations would call for ready forces to fight a holding action (these might do double duty for local wars), and measures to enlarge the mobilization base and to increase its security and the speed with which it can be converted. The accumulation of raw material stockpiles from overseas sources would be desirable, for example, in addition to securing the sea lanes. Construction of new capacity in industries that might "bottleneck" the expansion of war production, support of multiple sources of supply by expensive splitting of procurement contracts, and the training and maintenance of large reserve forces might be undertaken.

4. Cutting across all these areas, it would clearly be desirable to support a very large research and development effort. We are in an era in which a single technological mutation (as in the past, the development of radar and the atomic bomb) can far outweigh in military importance our substantial resources advantage. There are conceivable future mutations of equal importance—invulnerable long-range ballistic missiles, perhaps a high-confidence defense against nuclear weapons. Research and development is most obviously desirable in the context of thermonuclear wars: here certain kinds of technological slippage could break the stalemate, blunt deterrence, and place us at the mercy of the Kremlin. But it is also possible to conceive of developments which would, for example, greatly improve the capability of the United States to fight small engagements in out-of-the-way places. Development is cheap only by contrast with the procurement and maintenance of ready forces. If we tried to develop everything interesting (and possibly significant and therefore "desirable"), we could use all the potential as well as all the actual scientific and engineering resources of the country.

5. Finally, there are substantial opportunities to use economic strength in the cold war itself. Economic warfare, whether waged against our enemies or for our friends, can be expensive. It is widely believed that the Marshall Plan saved Western Europe from collapsing into chaos and perhaps Communism between 1947 and 1950, but at a cost of about 10 billion dollars. The United

States is now spending roughly a billion dollars a year on economic aid to friendly and neutral countries and the Soviet Union is lending over half a billion dollars annually, partly to its satellites and partly to other countries. Britain and Western Europe propose to spend many billions of dollars "uneconomically" on nuclear power plants to reduce their economic dependence on Middle Eastern oil, which is vulnerable both to Arab nationalism and to Soviet power. Economic strength permits a nation to wage the cold war more effectively, to reduce its vulnerability to hostile moves, and to improve its position and power by extending its influence.

These, then, are the desirable things—the things it would be nice to do from the point of view of national security. In the aggregate they far exceed our economic capabilities, so that hard choices must be made. But the greater our economic strength, the more desirable things we can do, and the better we can do them. We cannot prepare for all kinds of wars, but maybe we can prepare for more than one. We cannot develop every technological idea of promise, but maybe with three times Russia's economic strength we can develop enough more than she to keep ahead in the race for technological leadership. We cannot buy perfect protection against thermonuclear attack by any combination of active and passive defense, but perhaps we can afford enough defense to reduce Russian confidence of complete success to the point where she is deterred from striking. Perhaps on top of all this, we can afford a positive economic foreign policy which will preserve our alliances and increase our influence on developments in the uncommitted parts of the world.

At the least, the possession of greater economic strength enables us to do more of these things than we otherwise could do. But it does so if, and only if, we use the strength now, during the cold war, before a hot war starts. For that reason the term "economic war potential" will not be used in the present study. The timely translation of economic strength into military power, the proportion of that strength so translated, and the efficiency of the forces in being, have become of critical importance—as opposed to some theoretical maximum potential which could be translated into military force at some later date. While the traditional concept of the mobilization base is not yet fully obsolete and may even justify a limited expenditure of budget, it is no longer the shield of the Republic.

PART TWO

THE RESOURCES AVAILABLE FOR DEFENSE

III

RESOURCE LIMITATIONS

As noted earlier, Part I is devoted to problems of choice at comparatively high levels, choices among policies that affect (1) the resources at the nation's disposal and (2) the proportion of resources allocated to national defense. Our national security depends first of all upon these choices, for they determine the volume of resources available for defense.

Resource limitations are our starting point because in all problems of choice we strive to get the most out of what we have. To put it another way, we try to use the resources that are available to us so as to maximize what economists call "utility." Resources are always limited in comparison with our wants, always constraining our action. (If they did not, we could do everything, and there would be no problem of choosing preferred courses of action.) As a consequence, resource limitations are often called constraints. We try to achieve the most desirable outcome that is possible in view of these constraints.

We should therefore inquire into the nature of resource limitations as a preliminary step in selecting courses of action. In this chapter we shall discuss specific *versus* general resource constraints, the total resources that are at the nation's disposal; and policies that would influence those resources in the future. In subsequent chapters of Part II, we shall discuss how to choose the size of the defense budget and the major considerations bearing on that choice.

SPECIFIC VERSUS GENERAL CONSTRAINTS

How should constraints be expressed if they are to be most meaningful in appraising a nation's strength and in choosing the scale of the defense effort? What are the effective limitations on what we can do? Sometimes constraints are expressed as the projected supplies of specific items such as laborers in each skill and age bracket, tons of bauxite and mica, board feet of lumber, or kilowatt-hours of electricity. The supplies of individual items like these will be called "specific constraints." Sometimes, however, resource limitations are expressed as projected amounts of money that can be spent, putting a limit on the total effort but not on quantities of specific resources that can be employed. Such an over-all limitation will be called a "general constraint." In which form should constraints be expressed in different circumstances? In which form do they more accurately reflect the real limitations imposed by the physical world?

Different Constraints in Different Problems

In some problems, the constraints unquestionably ought to be expressed as definite quantities of specific products. Consider, for example, the decisions of a task force commander in a naval engagement. He must try to get the most from the particular items that are at his disposal—destroyers that are now in the force, man hours available for maintenance and operations, ammunition on hand, and so on. It is beside the point that, by allocating money in a budget differently, he could have equipped a task force with another aircraft carrier at a sacrifice of so many destroyers. The option of shifting basic resources from the production of one item to the production of another is hardly open at this stage of the game. Hence, in this situation, it is not a budget that constrains the actions of the commander. Limited stocks of specific items genuinely *are* the constraints, and they should be expressed in that fashion.

In other problems, however, the supplies of specific resources are not fixed, and the use of specific constraints is wrong. Consider the problems of the Navy in choosing next year's purchases of equipment. Of course, there will be some specific constraints—the physical impossibility, for example, of suddenly procuring an extraordinarily large quantity of some newly developed fuel or of completing an extra super carrier before a certain date. But one principal constraint will be the budget. Within the limits of this budget it will be physically possible to acquire varying amounts of many items—more training and less electronic gear, more ammunition and less manpower. In these circumstances, it *is* chiefly the budget that constrains: the Navy's supplies of many items are not fixed, and it would be wrong to choose policies as if they were.

Let us turn from the problems of naval planning for next year to problems of national policy over, say, the next decade. At first glance, the supplies of many basic resources may appear to be fixed. Manpower seems to be limited to its present size plus annual growth. Ore and petroleum reserves can hardly be manufactured. There is only so much coal to be mined. The acreage of each type of soil is already set. And yet, upon more careful inspection, one sees that the supplies of these resources that will be available in future periods are not really fixed. Medical programs and education can affect the total supply of labor. Through retraining, one kind of manpower can acquire a different skill. More intensive mining can recover a larger proportion of given ore reserves. A shift of resources can yield more metals at the expense of textiles or more titanium and less copper. The use of fertilizers, irrigation, drainage, tractors—these and many other innovations can alter the inventory of land, both in total and in composition.

Thus except in the very short run, the nation can usually get more of one item—even of many so-called basic resources, as far as future supplies are concerned—by sacrificing something else. The more distant the future to which the problem pertains, the less applicable are specific constraints. Where time and technology permit adjustments, the nation is not constrained by fixed supplies of individual resources, and thinking in terms of specific constraints is misleading. The real constraints, the truly "basic" resources, are exceedingly complex and difficult to measure, involving the state of the technological art, stocks of ingenuity and knowledge, institutional arrangements, and incentives as well as the total supplies of capital and people. Probably the most satisfactory way to represent these constraints is by means of some aggregate dollar amount of output that is at the nation's disposal each year. Such an amount, say national income or gross national product (GNP),[1] is a general constraint similar to a budget. It is a rough indicator of the aggregate output that is available annually, an indicator having no implication that the nation must work with specific quantities of individual items.

General monetary constraints are not put forward as perfect indicators of resource limitations even in the long run. Frequently some specific constraints will be operative as well as the general one (as in the case of the Navy's super carrier). Sometimes, too, specific limitations are imposed by decree of higher authority. For instance, the branches of the service, in planning ahead, face not only the general constraint of their budgets but also the specific

---

[1] Gross national product will be discussed in more detail in the next section of this chapter.

constraint of a manpower ceiling set by Congress. Strictly speaking, in problems of national policy as in most others, there is usually a combination of specific and general constraints.

Money Costs When General Constraints Apply

Only by counting the costs that constitute the real constraint can we determine the policies that achieve a specified task at minimum cost. If the stock of magnesium is the real constraint (and the only one), we should be interested in the cost of alternative actions in terms of magnesium. If several individual inputs are limited, we should be interested in the cost of alternative policies in terms of those inputs. If there is a general monetary constraint but specific inputs are not fixed, we should consider cost in dollars.[2]

To some people, dollars do not appear to reflect real resource cost, and their use has little appeal. Let us examine the justification for paying attention to monetary expense. What, in a fundamental sense, is the "cost" of a course of action? It is whatever must be given up in order to adopt that course, that is, whatever could otherwise be kept or obtained.[3] If we examine the problem of planning future programs from the standpoint of the Defense Department, it seems fairly obvious that money costs are pertinent. The Department faces a budgetary constraint. For the most part it does not face a limitation on particular weapons or supplies but can buy more of them by paying their prices. What does the Department give up in order to implement one course of action? The answer is money—or, to go one step further, the alternative weapons or supplies that could otherwise be purchased. The Department could substitute one item for another by paying the price of the one instead of paying the price of the other. Dollar costs do reflect what must be given up in order to adopt a particular policy. They reflect real sacrifices by the Department because the prices of different items show the rates at which they can be substituted for each other.

This is not to say that money costs perfectly represent resources sacrificed by the Defense Department. The prices of goods to be bought in the future are uncertain. One course of action may itself drive up the price of particular weapons or materials, and it is not possible to predict these effects with complete accuracy. The characteristics and cost of some items will change as technology advances. The quantity of some exceptional items may literally be

---

[2] Only by counting costs in these terms can we determine the policies that achieve the most with the given constraints, that is, with the available resources.

[3] That is, the cost is the sacrificed alternative *opportunity*. Hence, economists refer to these sacrificed alternatives as the "opportunity costs" of a course of action.

fixed, or nearly fixed, even if we are looking several years ahead. Nonetheless, imperfect as it is, the money cost of a future program usually shows the sacrifice that would be required of the Department better than other measures of cost. While dollars do not precisely measure the real sacrifices, costs in terms of metals and manpower would be grossly misleading. Saying that airplanes cost so much aluminum and ships so much steel plate does not tell us how one may be exchanged for the other. Saying that each costs so many dollars adheres more closely to the facts, namely, that the services can, in making future plans, trade one for the other.

But even if dollars reflect resource costs fairly well from the viewpoint of the Defense Department, do they do so from the standpoint of the nation? If the economy is a reasonably competitive one, the answer is Yes. The reason is that market prices in a competitive economy reflect not only the approximate rate at which the Defense Department can exchange one item for another but also the approximate rate at which the whole economy can substitute one article or material for another. Suppose that the price of a bomber is $1,000,000 and that of a destroyer $20,000,000. How can 20 bombers possibly entail the same resource cost as a destroyer? In other words, how can the construction of 20 bombers use up materials and manpower that could otherwise have produced one destroyer? Aircraft construction requires different metals, engineers with different skills, and different facilities from those required in shipbuilding. Obviously the set of inputs needed in the one case cannot be directly substituted for the other set of inputs. The specialist in aerodynamics cannot be put to work promptly and effectively on the design of destroyers. The labor force that might be used to build bombers in the Southwest cannot be shifted en masse to shipyards in Philadelphia.

Nonetheless, 20 bombers can use resources that would otherwise make it possible for the economy to produce one more destroyer. It is indirect substitution that makes this possible. If the bombers are ordered, the contractor must recruit the necessary laborers, build any newly required facilities, and buy the materials. In order to attract these resources, he will have to pay about what they could earn in their next-best use. These amounts or prices, in a competitive economy, correspond to the value of the output that the resources could otherwise produce. The sum of these amounts—the cost of the bombers—is therefore the value of civilian, or other, outputs that must be sacrificed.

As the recruitment of laborers and the purchase of materials takes place, a chain reaction is set off. The firms that begin to lose the laborers and materials try to replace them. The prices of aluminum, aeronautical engineers, and other resources used in aircraft production may rise somewhat relative to the prices of other inputs. Consumers of these scarcer resources shift to substitutes. Some workers learn that good jobs are available in aircraft plants and transfer to them, leaving vacancies in their former occupations, which in turn are attractive opportunities to still other workers. As a result of this process, the resources for the bombers are in effect released from myriad industries—perhaps coal-mining in Illinois, hair cutting in New Jersey, shrimp fishing in Louisiana —industries that are far removed from aircraft production.

Now suppose the destroyer is to be constructed instead of the airplanes. Imagine that we have a table model of the economy with figures to represent the various resources, and let us transfer the resources by hand. We do not move the men and materials directly from the aircraft industry to the shipyards. Instead we move them back to their next-best uses in the economy. The materials and men that would have replaced them in those uses are moved back in turn to their next-best uses. Simultaneously, we transfer resources into the production of destroyers, drawing them from other kinds of shipbuilding and related parts of the economy and setting off another sequence of shifts and substitutions.

If it is hard to take these roundabout substitutions seriously, remember that they happen constantly in real life. In any particular year some industries (for example, electronics or plastics) expand, and others (say, railroads or movies) decline. The growing industries, as a rule, take over few of the inputs once employed by the declining industries. Relative prices, reflecting the substitution possibilities among goods and services, lead firms to shift resources much more efficiently than transferring them directly from declining industries to expanding ones.[4]

As a consequence, money costs of *future* defense activities approximate the real alternatives that are foregone—the real sacrifices that are entailed—when one activity or weapon system is selected. This will be true for those problems in which a general monetary constraint is proper, that is, for problems pertaining to dates sufficiently in the future to permit the production and procurement of varying quantities of weapons and matériel.

---

[4] A more complete and rigorous discussion of these points can be found in most textbooks on the principles of economics, e.g., Paul Samuelson, *Economics*, 3d ed., New York, McGraw-Hill Book Co., 1955, pp. 17–21, 34–37, 49–50, 475–525.

GNP AS THE CONSTRAINT ON THE NATION'S ACTIVITIES

So far we have discussed the constraints and costs that are appropriate to defense problems or even problems in general. What about the problem at hand, that of assessing the nation's strength and deciding how much should be diverted to defense? By and large, in dealing with this problem, a general limitation on our efforts, such as GNP, is more nearly accurate and more useful than specific constraints. This problem is not how best to conduct a naval engagement with given weapons—not how to assess the power of a retaliatory attack that could be launched immediately. Instead the problem is how to gauge the strength that is the source of our defense effort and how to determine the share that should go to national security. These questions pertain to the planning of defense policies in future years, not to the planning of tactics for today's mission. There is time for a great deal of adjustment, and the constraint is more appropriately described as a general monetary one. It is more nearly correct to say that a projected $560-billion GNP (1957 dollars) will constrain our defense effort in 1965 than to say that 250,000 short-tons of magnesium, 150 billion ton-miles of transport, and 8 million long tons of sulfur will limit our program.

Moreover, even if particular resources were limited, a list of specific constraints would not be as manageable and meaningful as GNP in debating the above questions. Judgment as well as analysis must play an important role in assessing the nation's strength and deciding upon the share to be devoted to defense. These are questions that must be considered and debated at the highest levels—by the voters, by the administration in power, by the Congress. An electronic computer could take a large number of specific constraints and show a variety of combinations of output that could be produced. (It is scarcely possible, however, for a computer to show *all* of the combinations of output that could be produced with limitations of particular resources. Moreover, it is doubtful that such a tremendous mass of data would help anyone to reach better decisions about the national security budget.)[5] But the selection of the "correct" combination of defense and nondefense outputs depends greatly upon the unarticulated preferences of Congressmen and voters.

---

[5] This is *not* to say that electronic computers are unable to help us find useful answers to lower level problems of choice. On the contrary, they can help in many instances—as will be stressed in Part Three. For in many lower level problems, a suitable criterion can be made explicit, and calculations can point to the preferable courses of action.

That being the case, the resource limitations must be described in terms that the human mind can comprehend. It would be difficult, indeed impossible, for people to debate policy in the following manner: "In 1965 our strength will consist of 900 thousand short tons of fluorspar, 80 million man-years of labor, 15 thousand flasks of mercury (and so on). As the future situation looks to us now, the United States should plan on devoting 20 thousand tons of fluorspar, 20 million man-years of labor, and 2 thousand flasks of mercury to defense." It would surely be more meaningful to hear: "In 1965 our GNP will be 560 billion dollars. As the situation seems to shape up, the United States might plan on devoting 10 or 12 per cent of its GNP or roughly 60 to 70 billion dollars to national defense." For in the end, obligational authority and appropriations will be expressed in dollars, not in commodities. The debate about the scale of the military effort will take place mainly in terms of budgets (and the capabilities various budgets will buy), not in terms of commodities (and the weapons they can produce). Accordingly, as an aid in this debate, the constraint on the nation's activities—our economic strength—is most meaningful if it is expressed as a general monetary limitation.

Statements by government officials show that the debate usually does proceed in terms of a general monetary constraint, not only in appraising over-all strength but also specifically in deciding how many resources should be devoted to defense.[6] Right after the 1955 Geneva conference, former Secretary of Defense Wilson was reported as saying "he was considering whether more might not be spent on defense in the future if the national product and income continued to expand prosperously. To maintain the current level of defense spending in the face of a continually expanding economy, he suggested, would be tantamount to a cutback."[7] Thinking about defense expenditures in relation to GNP is not new. For example, President Truman in his 1952 Economic Report to the Congress stated, "Our total output [GNP], measured in 1951 prices, was more than 90 billion dollars higher than in 1939, and more than 100 billion above 1929. . . . The growth of production during the last few years now enables us to carry the security program without undue impairment of the rest of the economy."[8]

---

[6] See, for example, *Study of Airpower*, Hearings Before the Subcommittee on the Air Force of the Committee on Armed Services, U.S. Senate, 84th Congress, 2d Session, Part XXII, U.S. Government Printing Office, Washington, D.C., 1956, pp. 1668–72.

[7] *New York Times*, November 17, 1955, p. 11.

[8] *The Economic Report of the President*, together with a Report to the President, The Annual Economic Review, by the Council of Economic Advisers, Washington, D.C., 1952, p. 2.

For other problems, to be sure, other means of describing resource constraints are more pertinent. Suppose the problem is to select policies for industrial mobilization, as in World War II, rather than to choose the scale of the defense effort for cold or limited war. In that case, specific limitations are of the greatest significance. Thus, the programming of production in World War II depended upon the projected supplies of critical materials, skilled labor, and fabricated components (small electric motors, for example).[9] Because they were primarily concerned with the problems of industrial mobilization, previous books on the economics of defense have usually emphasized these limitations on individual resources.[10] But, as stressed earlier, the crucial problem in the nuclear era is not planning how best to mobilize our reserve strength. Instead the most urgent questions have to do with the planning of our forces in being for deterrence and limited conflicts. One of these questions is how much of our strength should be turned into forces in being. And for the purpose of attacking this question, we should think mainly in terms of a general monetary constraint.

The Meaning of GNP[11]

Gross national product, or GNP, is simply the dollar value of a nation's final output over a period of one year—about $440 billion in 1957 in the United States (1957 dollars). It is the total volume of goods and services, valued at market prices, that is at the nation's disposal over the period. Unlike net national income, GNP represents the whole of the nation's output, no portion being already set aside to allow for depreciation. Therefore any consumption, replacement of wornout or obsolete equipment, additions to the stock of capital, military outlays, or other government expenditures must come from GNP.[12] Of course, this measure is a proper constraint only if we are speaking of *full-employment* GNP. If only half the nation's resources are employed, GNP will be rela-

---

[9] See D. Novick, M. Anshen, and W. C. Truppner, *Wartime Production Controls*, Columbia University Press, New York, 1949.

[10] E.g., George A. Lincoln, *Economics of National Security*, 2nd ed., Prentice-Hall, Inc., New York, 1954 ; J. Blackman, A. Basch, S. Fabricant, M. Gainsbrugh, and E. Stein, *War and Defense Economics*, Rinehart & Co., Inc., New York, 1952; *Economic Mobilization and Stabilization*, L. V. Chandler and D. H. Wallace (eds.), Henry Holt and Co., New York, 1951; S. F. Harris, *The Economics of Mobilization and Inflation*, W. W. Norton & Co., Inc., New York, 1951.

[11] For a full decription of the concepts and methods used by the U.S. Government in measuring gross national product, see *National Income Supplement to the Survey of Current Business*, prepared in the Office of Business Economics of the U.S. Department of Commerce, U.S. Government Printing Office, Washington, D.C., 1954, pp. 27–158.

[12] For our present purpose, this statement is sufficiently accurate. It is not 100 per cent correct, for a nation could consume more than GNP for a time by drawing on inventories or on foreign balances, credits, or gifts.

tively small, but in those circumstances it is not a true indicator of the nation's capacity to produce. A larger defense program, or more of any program, can then be produced without sacrificing other things—simply by getting idle resources back to work. Thus the constraint referred to here is GNP at a high level of employment.

GNP is not the same thing as the total wealth of the nation—the value of its land, buildings, and equipment. The total wealth of the United States has been estimated to be about 800 billion dollars (as of 1948 and 1948 prices).[13] If the value of people as producers was counted among the country's assets, the figure would be much higher. But an estimate of the country's wealth is not directly pertinent to the problem of planning the national defenses. The assets of an individual or firm can be sold or "cashed in," and the proceeds can be devoted to any purpose that is chosen. Not so with the assets of the whole nation. They cannot be liquidated in order to get resources for defense or for any other purpose. The resources that can be devoted to national security are essentially the outputs that can be obtained each year from the stock of capital and supply of labor. Those are the outputs that make up GNP. If all of GNP is consumed, the capital stock is slowly depleted. If part of it is invested, capital may be maintained or augmented. But GNP is the amount that is at our disposal over a year's time.

If each year's GNP is expressed in current prices, it will reflect changes in the general price level, that is, inflation or deflation. If it is expressed in terms of a constant price level, GNP is an index of the physical volume of final output. When talking about past years, it is often proper to refer to GNP in current dollars, since past defense budgets too are ordinarily in current dollars. When considering future national-security policies, however, there is no reason to introduce the capricious effects of changes in the general price level. Our concern is either with the relationship between the defense budget and GNP or with physical output in "constant" dollars. In discussing future GNP and future budgets, we should think of the amounts in constant dollars.[14]

It should be noted that GNP includes government expenditures for goods and services as though this amount measured accurately

---

[13] Raymond Goldsmith, "A Perpetual Inventory of National Wealth," *Studies in Income and Wealth,* Vol. 14, National Bureau of Economic Research, New York [no date], p. 18.

[14] Whether to use GNP valued at market prices or by an "adjusted factor cost standard" depends partly upon the precise problem that is being considered. See Abram Bergson, *Soviet National Income and Product in 1937,* Columbia University Press, New York, 1953, pp. 42–54. For the United States (where indirect business taxes are small compared to their amount in, say, the USSR) it probably makes little difference which of the two is used. Unless otherwise specified, we will refer in this study to GNP valued at market prices.

the value of the government's final product. Two major objections to this procedure are widely recognized: (1) This is not a satisfying measurement of the value of government output. The government's services may be worth either more or less than their cost. (2) Part of the government's output, for example, statistical services, may be regarded as intermediate products—that is, as ingredients of private output whose value is already counted. Why, then, do our national income accounts continue to use expenditures to represent the final product in government? The answer is simply that this procedure, rough as it is, appears to be better than the practicable alternatives.

There are other difficulties with the concept and measurement of GNP.[15] There are questions particularly about the extent to which such measurements can reflect ultimate national well-being. But these difficulties need not detain us. Even if it does not measure total satisfaction or welfare accurately, full-employment GNP appears to be a useful index of physical production possibilities—a useful indicator of the flow from which resources for national defense must be diverted.

There is another aspect of GNP that should be kept in mind. Earlier it was pointed out that unique outputs of specific items cannot properly be regarded as fixed constraints. GNP as observed and measured, even with full employment, is not absolutely invariant either. Later in this chapter, methods of stimulating the growth of GNP will be mentioned. But quite apart from long-term growth, there is a certain amount of short-run resiliency—of quick expansion that can be achieved by taking up the slack. For example, at the outbreak of the Korean conflict, the nation was experiencing what one might call normal full employment. Yet in 1951 the 20-billion-dollar increase in annual defense expenditures was accompanied by a 20-billion-dollar increase in real national income, an amount of growth almost triple the amount that could ordinarily be expected. As a consequence, instead of the drastic price-level inflation anticipated by many persons, there was a sharp increase in real production—the military services using more output without reducing the nation's consumption or investment—and only a modest inflation. Part of this increment in output was no doubt illusory—attributable to flaws in the measurements. But not all of it. How did the increase in the defense budget produce this

---

[15] Examples are the difficulties in handling non-marketed outputs and changes in the quality of products. For discussions of these and other points, see *A Critique of the United States Income and Product Accounts*, Studies in Income and Wealth, Vol. 22, A Report of the National Bureau of Economic Research, Princeton University Press, Princeton, N.J., 1958.

effect? Presumably by offering larger lures, causing people to work harder and longer, attracting additional persons into the labor force, bringing more rapid application of technological improvements, and altering the composition of output. Thus, projected full-employment GNP is not an absolutely inflexible limitation on output.[16] Nevertheless, it is a good approximate indicator of the over-all constraint on the nation's activities.

It should be noted too that while GNP is a useful index of resource limitations, it is no simple matter to divert GNP from consumption to defense, or investment. On the contrary, it is a difficult thing to do, particularly in a free democratic society. J. K. Galbraith has pointed this out very forcefully in his book, *The Affluent Society*.[17] Most of the growth of the United States, for instance, stems from increases in consumption and from private investment designed to meet consumers' demands. Interdependence makes it technically difficult for us to give up the use of certain items (even the family's second car) that may appear to be frills; and our emphasis on consumption makes it psychologically difficult for us to sacrifice such items.

Consequently, according to Galbraith, the "minimum" standard of living is always the existing one, and no Administration or Congress that is interested in being reelected is likely to propose any substantial reduction in that standard of living. In this connection, it may be significant that the United States devoted mainly "slack" or growth to World War II and the Korean conflict; in neither instance was the absolute level of consumption (as usually measured) reduced.

We must therefore avoid identifying GNP, or even expected growth of GNP, with economic strength for the cold war. It is an illusion to think that the United States can twist a faucet and convert its mighty GNP into deterrent capability without a change in popular value-judgments. It takes both GNP and willingness to make sacrifices to yield resources *for national defense*.

Determinants of GNP

As mentioned earlier, the truly basic resources include not only the supplies of capital and people but also institutional arrange-

---

[16] For an attempt to allow for the extra capacity that would come to light if expanded defense spending caused the nation to produce under pressure, see Gerhard Colm and Manuel Helzner, "General Economic Feasibility of National Security Programs," National Planning Association, March 20, 1957, published in *Federal Expenditure Policy for Economic Growth and Stability*, Hearings before the Subcommittee on Fiscal Policy of the Joint Economic Committee, 85th Congress, 1st Session, U.S. Government Printing Office, Washington, D.C., 1958, pp. 359-360.

[17] J. K. Galbraith, *The Affluent Society*, Houghton Mifflin Company, Boston, 1958, pp. 161-180 (Chapter XII on "The Illusion of National Security".)

ments, incentives, and the state of the technological art. Such factors are the underlying determinants that one may consider when trying to estimate future GNP or to figure out policies that can increase it. The principal determinants are summarized in the following list.[18]

A. Initial Stock of Basic Resources and Their Use
  1. Manpower
     a. Labor
     b. Number of hours in the work-week
     c. Level of employment
     d. Extent of skill and training
  2. Stock of capital equipment
  3. State of the art and knowledge
  4. Degree of efficiency in the use of resources
     a. Allocation of resources among uses
     b. Methods of organization to make use of our knowledge
     c. Incentives to produce

B. Growth
  1. Increase in manpower
     a. Increases in the labor force
     b. Changes in the work-week
     c. Changes in the level of employment
     d. Improvement in skills and training
  2. Growth of capital stock
  3. Advances in the state of the art
     a. Amount of resources devoted to research and education
     b. Incentives to explore new ideas
  4. Efficiency in taking advantage of innovations
     a. Incentives to introduce innovations
     b. Mechanism for reshuffling resources in response to innovations.

Most of these items and their relation to the nation's potential output are self-explanatory. Thus, the pertinence of manpower, capital equipment (for example, machines, buildings, and other structures), and the state of the art (for example, knowledge of hybrid corn or transistors) is probably clear. The role of efficiency

---

[18] For other lists of growth determinants and discussions of them, see M. Abramovitz, "Economics of Growth," in *A Survey of Contemporary Economics*, Vol. II, Richard D. Irwin, Inc., Homewood, Ill., 1952, especially pp. 132–144; W. Arthur Lewis, *The Theory of Economic Growth*, George Allen & Unwin, Ltd., London, 1955; *Capital Formation and Economic Growth*, A Conference of the Universities-National Bureau Committee for Ecoonmic Research, Princeton University Press, Princeton, N.J., 1955; W. W. Rostow, *The Process of Economic Growth*, The Clarendon Press, Oxford, 1953.

in the use of these resources, however, may need to be clarified. Without suitable incentives and a reasonable allocation of its resources, a nation can fall short of getting maximum output from its manpower, capital, and "laboratory knowledge." If monopoly, governmental restriction, tax structures, or other "institutions" impair incentives or discourage resources from moving to their best uses, the potential GNP of the nation will not be fulfilled.

Such factors can also operate to promote or retard long-run growth of GNP. The institutional framework undoubtedly has much to do with advances in the state of the art. In one environment, inventiveness flourishes; in another, it languishes. Moreover, even after new ideas are conceived, the institutional framework influences the rate at which innovations are made and diffused and the speed with which resources are subsequently reshuffled.[19] If monopolistic restrictions, financial organization, or government policies tend to shelter the status quo, known technological improvements may not spread rapidly, and resources may not shift quickly to what now become their best uses.

One wonders, naturally enough, about the quantitative significance of these various factors. Are some of them, such as incentives and institutional framework, merely high-sounding abstractions that actually exert little influence on the growth of GNP? Does it turn out, upon close inspection, that the rise of GNP is accounted for almost solely by the increase in capital equipment and the labor force? Or does it turn out that the other factors do play a major part in economic growth?

Recent studies have begun to shed light on the answers to these questions. These studies indicate that the rise of GNP in the United States has far outstripped the growth in the quantities of capital and labor.[20] More specifically, they suggest that half or more of the increase in national product must be attributed to rising productivity of the inputs. One researcher concludes that "Of the historic increase in GNP, about half represented the effect of

---

[19] The effects of institutions on the growth of knowledge, the application of new ideas, and the reshuffling of resources have attracted a good deal of attention in recent years. For provocative discussions, see W. Arthur Lewis, pp. 1–200; Yale Brozen, "Business Leadership and Technological Change," *American Journal of Economic and Sociology*, Vol. 14, pp. 13–30; and Yalt Brozen, "Invention Innovation, and Imitation," *American Economic Review*, Papers and Proceedings, XLI, May 1951, pp. 239–257.

[20] M. Abramovitz, "Resource and Output Trends in the United States since 1870," *American Economic Review*, Papers and Proceedings, XLVI, May 1956, pp. 5–23, reprinted by the National Bureau of Economic Research as Occasional Paper No. 52; John W. Kendrick, "Productivity Trends: Capital and Labor," *Review of Economics and Statistics*, XXXVIII, August 1956, pp. 248–257, reprinted by the National Bureau as Occasional Paper No. 53; Jacob Schmookler, "The Changing Efficiency of the American Economy: 1869–1938," *Review of Economics and Statistics*, XXXIV, August 1952, pp. 214–231.

increased resources, and half, the effect of increased efficiency of resource use." [21] According to another inquiry, an index of factor inputs (capital and labor combined) quadrupled between the decade of 1869–78 and that of 1944–53, while over the same period net national product grew to 13 times its original size.[22] Such results indicate that new ideas and their efficient and widespread application may be of overriding importance to growth.

This conclusion apparently applies with as much force to "underdeveloped" countries as it does to the United States:

> The per capita output of the United States rose at a rate of about 1.9 per cent per year (compounded) of which only about one-tenth is ascribed to the rise in the stock of tanglible capital, according to Fabricant.[23] The rest of this remarkable economic growth may be represented as coming from increases in output per unit of input of labor and of such capital.
>
> Such fragmentary data as there are for Latin-American countries indicate the same pattern. In Mexico, for example, the relatively large crop producing sector increased its output 60 per cent from 1925–29 to 1945–49, using, however, only 27 per cent more input; thus output per unit of aggregate input rose by 26 per cent. Farm production in Brazil was 55 per cent larger in 1945–49 than in 1925–29. The input index rose only 30 per cent; and, accordingly, output per unit of aggregate input increased 20 per cent.[24]

Such data do not show just what influence is exerted on economic growth by each factor, but they do suggest that, to achieve rapid growth, an economy needs more than a growing supply of tools and labor. It needs education and investment in human beings, research, and an environment in which inventiveness is stimulated, and a framework in which the reshuffling of resources is permitted. Both new discoveries and untrammeled adjustment afterward seem to be important to rapid growth. On the one hand, inventions cannot be applied unless they are discovered, and, on the other hand, the fruits of inventions cannot be harvested unless they are widely applied and resources are efficiently reallocated. Consider the effects of a single innovation—atomic power. Suppose that atomic power made the cost of electricity 2½

---

[21] Schmookler, p. 224.

[22] Abramovitz, p. 8.

[23] Solomon Fabricant, "Economic Progress and Economic Change" (a part of the 34th Annual Report of the National Bureau of Economic Research, May, 1954). Tangible capital here consists of structures, including housing, equipment, inventories and net foreign assets, but excluding consumer equipment, military assets and land and subsoil assets [footnote from passage quoted].

[24] Clarence A. Moore, "Agricultural Development in Mexico," *Journal of Farm Economics*, February, 1955; Clarence A. Moore, "Agricultural Development in Brazil" (unpublished TALA paper, No. 54–044, September 29, 1954, University of Chicago) [footnote of T. W. Schultz, author of the passage quoted]; Theodore W. Schultz, "Latin-American Economic Policy Lessons," *American Economic Review*, Papers and Proceedings, XLVI, May 1956, pp. 430–431.

mills per kilowatt hour less than it would otherwise be. It has been estimated that our national income would be increased by no more than 2/5 of 1 percent.[25] Even this growth could occur only if there was considerable readjustment in the economy. And only if "trigger effects" (the impacts of further innovations that emerge as firms try to take advantage of atomic power)[26] were introduced— only then could the projected increase in national income become very impressive. Without the trigger effects, most great inventions—the printing press, the railroad, the internal combustion engine—would surely have made only modest contributions to total production. Hence, not only institutions that stimulate research and inventiveness but also those that facilitate full adjustment by the economy are influential factors in economic growth.

GNP, Past and Future

So much for the meaning of GNP and its determinants. How has this index to the nation's strength read in recent years? How do recent readings compare with those of earlier years? What are the prospects that lie ahead?

In 1957, GNP amounted to $440 billion. Of this final output of $440 billion, $284 billion or 65 percent was devoted to personal consumption, $65 billion or 15 per cent to gross private domestic investment, and $47 billion or 11 percent to national security. (The remainder was net foreign investment and other government purchases of goods and services.)

Compare these figures with the corresponding amounts for earlier years. In 1953, when United States expenditures on the Korean conflict were at their peak, we produced a gross national product of $399 billion and devoted $60 billion or 15 percent to national security programs. In 1929, GNP was only $197 billion, and national security expenditures were less than one per cent.[27]

---

[25] Herbert A. Simon, "The Effects of Atomic Power on National or Regional Economics," chapter XIII in Sam H. Schurr and Jacob Marschak, *Economic Aspects of Atomic Power*, Princeton University Press, Princeton, N.J., 1950. For the assumptions that guided the preparation of these exploratory estimates, see that volume and particularly chapter XIII.

[26] *Ibid.*, pp. 232–234.

[27] All the amounts and calculations in this section are in terms of 1957 dollars. The amounts in 1954 dollars are given in the *Survey of Current Business*, July 1958, pp. 10–11. They were converted to 1957 dollars by using the implicit deflators published in the same source. For more precise measurements, this method of putting the amounts in 1957 dollars would be too rough, but for our purposes the procedure seems to be suitable.

National security expenditures in current dollars for 1941 to 1957 (*Ibid.*, pp. 4–5) were converted to 1957 dollars by using the implicit deflators for federal purchases of goods and services. For 1929 to 1940, inclusive, national security outlays were approximated in the following way: For those years, military expenditures as a percentage of military plus civil governmental expenditures have been estimated (M. Slade Kendrick, *A Century and a Half of Federal Expenditures*. Occasional Paper No. 48, National Bureau of Economic Research, New York, 1955, p. 41). These factors were applied to "federal purchases of goods and services" (roughly equivalent to the National Bureau's "military plus civil" expenditures) in 1957 dollars.

As for future years, the President's Materials Policy Commission has estimated that GNP can rise at a rate of about 3 percent per year, at least for the next few decades.[28] In making the projections, the Commission's staff tried to take into consideration the determinants of GNP that were discussed above. Looking at 1975 (really "a shorthand means of denoting 'sometime in the 1970's' "), the Commission assumed a labor force of 82 million people. This figure rested on an estimate that there would be 146 million people 14 years of age and over, with the labor force constituting, as at present, 56 percent of that number. Of this supply of laborers, 4 million were expected to be in the military service, 7½ million in agriculture, and 2½ million unemployed. Another assumption was that the average work week would decline 15 percent by the middle 70's. Finally, with our institutional arrangements, the probable growth of the capital stock, and advances in technology, it was believed that productivity (average output per man-hour) would rise at a rate of 2½ percent per year. The resulting rate of growth would yield a GNP of $700 billion—over 50 percent greater than that of 1957—by the middle 1970's.

Figure 1 shows the past and projected growth of GNP, and the past allocations to national security, consumption, and private domestic investment. National security outlays, it might be noted, include the programs for atomic energy, stockpiling, and Mutual Defense Assistance, as well as the strictly military programs. As can be seen in the figure, GNP has increased rapidly during the past two decades, and can continue to grow at about the same rate. While personal consumption has not quite kept pace with this rate of growth, national security outlays have risen from nearly nothing to about 10 percent of GNP. Note, however, that national security expenditures constituted a smaller part of the total in 1957 than they did during either the Korean War or World War II. Table I traces these components as percentages of gross national product.

If we merely continue to devote 10 per cent to national security, the absolute amount could reach $70 billion in 1957 dollars by the early 1970's. And if the national security program became 15 percent of GNP (over $100 billion in 1957 dollars), consumption and investment could still expand tremendously. In other words, production possibilities are likely to increase greatly over the next

---

[28] *Resources for Freedom*, A Report to the President by the President's Materials Policy Commission, Vol. II, U.S. Government Printing Office, Washington, D.C., 1952, pp. 111–12. Most efforts to project GNP have produced similar estimates; see, for example, Committee for Economic Development, *Economic Growth in the United States, Its Past and Future*, A Statement on National Policy by the Research and Policy Committee. February 1958, pp. 42–43.

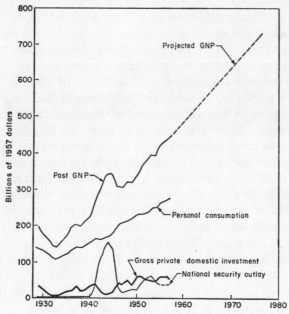

*Figure 1.   GNP and major components, 1929–1957; and projected
GNP, 1958–1975.*

Table 1.   *Major Components as Percentages of GNP in Selected Years*

Compounds	Percentages of GNP					
	1930	1940	1944	1950	1953	1957
Personal consumption	71	68	49	66	62	65
Gross private domestic investment	15	15	4	19	15	15
National security	1	1	46	7	15	11
Other	13	16	1	8	8	9

two decades, easing the constraint on these various activities. If
we view this future growth from the vantage point of, say, the
early 1960's, we still have considerable latitude in choosing how
this extra output is to be used.

ALTERNATIVE POLICIES AFFECTING FUTURE RESOURCES

Future GNP is not irrevocably determined. It does not have to
behave in accordance with projections like those shown above.

Quite apart from errors of estimation, GNP may deviate from its projected path on account of either fortuitous events or deliberate policies. In this section, the possibilities of deliberately increasing future resources will be mentioned. They will not be examined in detail, for the primary concern of this study is defense, not general economic growth. But it is relevant not only to take existing resource constraints into account but also to consider at least briefly the means of influencing future constraints.

Even in the short run when the supply of resources is given, government policies can affect the level of employment and the efficiency with which the resources are employed. Monetary-fiscal policy to avoid the unemployment that comes with recession can be of enormous significance. During the thirties, to take an extreme example, the loss of GNP due to unemployment was "some 300 billion dollars—almost equal to the real economic cost of World War II." [29] Recession could severely reduce our strength without being anything like the deep depression of the 1930's. Of course, the actual GNP that occurs when there is large-scale unemployment is not properly a constraint on defense activities, for resources can then be put into defense programs without sacrificing other outputs. Nonetheless, in reducing our economic strength and pulling down the economies of our allies, recession would seriously undermine our national security. Moreover, recession would shrink investment, retard technological advance, and stunt the future growth of GNP, resulting in more confining resource limitations at a later date than would otherwise exist. We should make no mistake on this point—a sharp recession could curtail ominously the economic basis for national security planning. Therefore the government should be willing to cut taxes, expand the volume of money, and reduce interest rates if aggregate demand slumps and serious unemployment develops. We should keep up our guard against overconfidence in "new-era" psychology.

It would be wrong, however, in trying to avoid recession, to invite drastic inflation. Deficits and easy money in *all* circumstances are not the answer. For severe inflation too prevents the economy from functioning efficiently and retards its development. It frequently leads to price controls, which inhibit the market mechanism, because people object to its inequities. Furthermore, violent inflation (or any inflation suppressed by price controls) pushes people into inefficient activities such as barter and efforts to convert monetary receipts into goods immediately. Hyperinflation usually ends with the economy thoroughly disorganized.

---

[29] Samuelson, *Economics*, p. 225.

Thus, among the government actions that are vitally important to GNP and its growth are monetary-fiscal efforts to guide aggregate demand for goods and services—to steer the economy between the Scylla of deflation and the Charybdis of inflation.

Other government policies affect the efficiency with which given resources are used, thus influencing the size of GNP. On the one hand, restrictions on firms and individuals, though stemming from the best of intentions, may distort the allocation of resources and impair incentives. Price controls, price supports, minimum wage laws, tariffs, and subsidies often produce such distortions. On the other hand, failure to intervene in certain situations allows distortions to persist. Examples are situations in which monopolistic groups can restrict entry into occupations or industries, or situations in which firms do not bear certain costs that they inflict on others (for example, by polluting water or congesting highways). In addition to their influence on the efficiency of the private economy, public policies determine the efficiency with which the government's own activities are conducted.

It is inappropriate here to describe specific policies that would yield increased efficiency in the private and public sectors of the economy. We will, however, stress one point. In order to choose the specific actions that constitute preferred policies, policy-makers need analytical assistance wherever it can be provided. They need well-conceived estimates of the prospective gains and costs of alternative courses of action. Without such estimates, advice is bound to consist of generalities and to sound arbitrary, or like an exhortation to do good. To say anything concrete about the merits of, say, a particular subsidy, the costs and gains from alternative arrangements must be estimated. To make recommendations about a particular health program, the costs and effects have to be gauged, albeit roughly. To choose the government investments that will contribute most to future GNP, the impacts of alternative investments must be measured as best we can. Systematic effort to determine preferred courses of action is called "operations research" when applied to problems in military or industrial operations. It is called "systems analysis" when applied to certain broader or longer-range problems, particularly the comparison of weapons systems. It is called "cost-benefit analysis" when such things as water-resource developments are being considered. More and better analysis may be useful in increasing efficiency in shaping many government programs and policies.[30] And increased

---

[30] Roland N. McKean, *Efficiency in Government through Systems Analysis*, John Wiley and Sons, New York, 1958.

effectiveness in shaping these policies means higher GNP and greater growth—a larger resource base for defense and all the other activities that contribute to the national well-being.

In the longer run, when the supplies of capital, labor, and knowledge can be expanded, there are additional methods of increasing future GNP. While this country would hardly attempt to control the quantity of labor, government policies may affect the evolution of the work week and will definitely influence the health, education, training, and mobility of our manpower. This form of investment, that is, in human resources, probably yields a comparatively high return.[31] National policy can also influence the volume of private investment in capital equipment and, more directly, the volume of public investment. Private capital formation depends, in part, upon monetary-fiscal policies because they affect the availability of funds, upon the size and character of the government budget because some public spending competes with private spending and other public spending stimulates it, upon the tax structure because some taxes deter investment more than others. Public capital formation, of course, is determined by the proportion of the budget that is devoted to investment.

Another means of shaping economic development is by devoting more funds to basic research and exploratory development, and, of course, by maintaining a free economy in which the fruits of discoveries can best be harvested. The government sponsors a good deal of research at present, much of it as part of the national security programs, but the payoff to the nation from still more research appears to be high. Such evidence as adding up the direct results of a few outstanding developments tends to support this conclusion.[32] Although it is extremely hard to measure the returns attributable to research, the average annual return on this form of investment has been estimated to be from 100 to 200 per cent.[33] Calculations have been made which suggest the same general range in one sector of the economy, agriculture. The savings in 1950 due to improvements in production techniques from 1940 to 1950 have been estimated at 60 to 300 per cent (lower and upper

[31] Theodore W. Schultz, *Redirecting Farm Policy*, Macmillan Co., New York, 1943, pp. 68–71.

[32] For example, see *The Mighty Force of Research* by the Editors of *Fortune*, McGraw-Hill Book Co., Inc., New York, 1956; Yale Brozen, "The Economic Future of Research and Development," *Industrial Laboratories*, Vol. 4, December 1953, pp. 5–8; Allen Abrams, "Measuring the Return from Research," Proceedings of the Fourth Annual Conference on the Administration of Research, University of Michigan, Ann Arbor, 1951; and Zvi Griliches, "Research Costs and Social Returns: Hybrid Corn and Related Innovations," *Journal of Political Economy*, October 1958, pp. 419–431.

[33] This was the estimate of Raymond Ewell of the National Science Foundation—mentioned in *The Mighty Force of Research*, p. vi.

limits) of ten years' research and extension outlays at the 1950 rate of expenditure.[34]

A substantial amount of government activity in this sphere, particularly in basic research, seems to be justified. Research that is profitable to the whole economy may nonetheless be unprofitable to any individual firm, because the gains are so widely diffused. Such research must usually be sponsored by universities, foundations, or government agencies.

There are several ways in which defense policy can itself affect resources available in the future. National-security programs may have by-product effects on the determinants of GNP, for instance, on the employment level or the rate of technological advance, Also, the efficiency of defense activities can influence the resources that will be available in the future by affecting the amount that the nation can devote to investment.

SUMMARY

In the very short run (say in a military situation in which a commander must use the specific forces at his disposal), resource constraints are properly viewed as quantities of specific inputs. In the longer run, in decisions affecting the situation several years hence, the main resource limitations are best viewed as general monetary constraints, and costs are best measured as dollar costs.

In connection with longer-run decisions, the over-all constraint on the nation's consumption, investment, defense, and other activities can be regarded as the nation's capacity to produce as measured by full-employment GNP (gross national product). Only for very sudden and drastic changes in the level and composition of such activities would it be either helpful or necessary to think in terms of specific resource constraints.

GNP in the United States is likely to increase a great deal over the coming decades, offering considerable freedom of choice in determining the amounts to be devoted to defense (and the other categories of expenditure). Moreover, national policies, including defense planning itself, can affect the growth of the nation's resources.

---

[34] Theodore W. Schultz, "Agricultural Research: Expenditures and Returns," in *The Economic Organization of Agriculture*, McGraw-Hill Book Co., Inc., New York, 1953, pp. 114–122. If we look at a longer period, savings in 1950 due to improvements from 1910 to 1950 are from 130 to 230 per cent of 40 years' research and extension outlays at the 1950 rate of expenditure.

IV

DIVERTING GNP TO DEFENSE:
HOW BIG A DEFENSE BUDGET?

Defense expenditures in the late 1950's have set new records for peacetime, outlays for military plus other major national security activities amounting to over 40 billion dollars annually. Budgets of this size, naturally enough, are viewed with considerable concern. Have the added outlays in recent years purchased things that were worth the cost? Or has spending just become a "happy reflex?" [1] How much of GNP should be devoted to defense? Before we take up such questions, or try to show how they should be approached, let us review a few points about the formulation of the budget in the United States.

THE BUDGETARY PROCESS [2]

The annual defense budget is part of the massive document, *The Budget of the United States,* which the President sends to Congress each January. An enormous amount of time, effort, and "bargaining" goes into its preparation.

Consider the military budget for the fiscal year 1960 (July 1959 to July 1960). Part of the work on these estimates was started about two years earlier—that is, in mid-1957. At about that time [3] the departments of the Army, Navy, and Air Force began to plan for the fiscal year 1960. They based their figures on the force requirements and long-range plans tentatively established at various levels in the Executive branch. On the basis of directives from the top levels of the Army, Navy, and Air Force, the lower levels worked up detailed programs showing the physical inputs that would be "required."

---

[1] Senator Paul Douglas has wondered if people are now conditioned so that their mouths water when budget-time rolls around much as Dr. Pavlov's dogs began to salivate when a bell was rung.

[2] For a detailed account, see Arthur Smithies, *The Budgetary Process in the United States,* McGraw-Hill Book Company, New York, 1955, pp. 101–159 and 240–256. We are indebted to Frederick M. Sallagar of The RAND Corporation for several of the points stressed in this section.

[3] The procedures are constantly evolving, and they vary from one department to the next; the statements here depict a sort of "average" procedure that may not be one hundred per cent correct for any particular department over any particular budget cycle.

Next, in the spring and summer of 1958, these programs were modified, costed, and converted into departmental budgets. Early in this period, the Secretary of Defense issued "budget guidelines" to the individual Services. Then the budget offices of the departments issued their "calls for estimates," and the various commands and bureaus prepared budget estimates. During the summer the departmental budget offices sent preliminary budgets to the Secretary of Defense. At this point the Secretary discussed the figures with the President and with officials in the Bureau of the Budget. After some further revision, perhaps on the basis of Presidential ceilings, the estimates were sent to the Budget Bureau.

During the autumn of 1958, these figures were revised by the Budget Bureau and also by the Defense Department. A series of discussions involving officials in the individual departments, the Defense Department, and the Budget Bureau took place. The Secretary of Defense, after consulting with the Chief of Staff and each departmental secretary, officially transmitted the estimates to the Budget Bureau. The latter sent its recommendations to the President. In January 1959, the President, having reached final decisions, submitted the official document to Congress along with his budget message. (Sample exhibits, taken from the budget for the fiscal year 1960, are shown later in the chapter.)

Finally, the stage that we usually read about in the papers was reached. During the spring and early summer of 1959 there were the hearings before the subcommittees of the Committee on Appropriations, the Congressional debates, and the passage of appropriations bills for the fiscal year 1960 by both the House and the Senate. (At the same time, the Services were trying to adjust their programs to make them consistent with the revisions in their budgets.)

Thus, budget formulation is a long and complex process, and the results are influenced considerably by the mechanics and institutions involved. It is a process of bargaining among officials and groups having diverse strengths, aims, convictions, and responsibilities. Also, these participants naturally have various "political" considerations in mind—concerns about the impact of budgetary decisions on the success of rival departments or officials, on the attitudes of voters, on the actions of various groups. The effects, as far as reaching sound decisions is concerned, are not all bad—nor are they all good.

Other notable characteristics of the process are oppressive deadlines and inadequate opportunities for decision-makers to study exhibits. At best, officials can hardly give attention to the issues commensurate with their importance. Both civilian and military administrators have other day-to-day decisions to make, multitudes of them. If we ask ourselves how we would prepare or evaluate this thousand-page document or the hundred-page portion pertaining to the Defense Department, we can better appreciate the awesome nature of this task.

Moreover, there is often severe personal penalty for originating mistakes yet little or no penalty for perpetuating past decisions—except in time of crisis. Consequently there are strong forces against making "new" decisions (in budget formulation as well as in other governmental problems of choice) except when palpable crises occur.

In brief, deciding upon the defense budget is a tremendous task that must be performed under difficult circumstances. We cannot expect to identify or achieve "optimal" solutions; we should have no illusions on this score. Nonetheless, looking at the problem in the right way can aid us in reaching better solutions. It can help officials get better results with existing institutions—and it may point toward institutional modifications that can improve budgetary decision.

BUDGET-FIRSTERS VERSUS NEED-FIRSTERS

To get the most out of the nation's resources, we devote fewer billions to national security if some defense activities are worth less to the nation than they cost, and spend still more billions if extra defenses would yield greater value than the other things that the money could buy. This way of looking at the problem is not universally accepted, however. Some persons apparently believe that the size of the national security program should be determined in the light of cost alone. They name some figure and say "That's all we'll pay, and that's that." Others apparently believe that the program should be planned on the basis of need alone. In Congressional hearings, military leaders are often asked to reveal what they "really need." For instance, Senator Chavez told General Maxwell D. Taylor, "We would like to know what you need and not what the Budget Bureau thinks you should have." [4] As another case in point, Senator Ervin deplored the Defense Department's willingness to cut purchases below our "needs." According to the Senator, this attitude smacked of the economic

---

[4] *Department of Defense Appropriations for 1957*, Hearings Before the Subcommittee of the Committee on Appropriations, U.S. Senate, 84th Congress, 2d Session, U.S. Government Printing Office, Washington, D.C., 1956, p. 93.

philosophy of an old acquaintance who used to say, "Now, good boy, if you want to get along in this world you just have to do without the things you have to have." [5]

Some simply say that the task of determining budget size has to be done one way or the other:

> In general, there are two ways in which the problem of balancing defense needs against fiscal requirements can be approached. One way is to ascertain essential defense needs and then see if the funds can be made available to meet them. The other is to predetermine, as a matter of fiscal policy, a dollar limit for defense expenditures; and thereupon refuse to satisfy any defense needs that cannot be compressed within that limit.[6]

The truth is, however, that one cannot properly draw up defense plans on the basis of either cost alone or needs alone. There is no budget size or cost that is correct regardless of the payoff, and there is no need that should be met regardless of cost.

On the one hand, there is no presumption that the defense budget is now, or should be, near any immovable upper limit. As far as physical and economic feasibility is concerned, national security expenditures could be raised (within a two- or three-year transition period) by, say, $30 billion per year. With appropriate changes in tax rates and monetary policy, this could be done without causing severe inflation.

From existing levels, in other words, outlays for defense activities can be raised if we really want to raise them—if we feel that we need extra defense programs more than other things. There is, of course, a maximal amount that could be devoted to national security. It is less than total GNP, since part must go for subsistence and supporting activities in order to have any security program at all. But there is no magic number like fifty or seventy-five or one hundred billion dollars which we can stand, and above which we can't. To be sure, the larger the budget, the greater the sacrifice, but we cannot say, as some have tried to argue, that taxes amounting to more than 25 per cent of national income must inevitably bring collapse or intolerable inflation.[7] Countries in Western Europe have successfully borne taxes in excess of 30 per cent of GNP.

---

[5] *Study of Airpower*, Hearings Before the Subcommittee on the Air Force of the Committee on Armed Services, U.S. Senate, 84th Congress, 2d Session, Part XXII, U.S. Government Printing Office, Washington, D.C., 1956, p. 1691.

[6] *Airpower*, Report of the Subcommittee on the Air force of the Committee on Armed Services, U.S. Senate, 84th Congress, U.S. Government Printing Office, Washington, D.C., 1957, p. 9.

[7] For example, Colin Clark took such a position, often cited, in "Public Finance and Changes in the Value of Money," *Economic Journal*, December 1945, pp. 371-389.

We shall not try to add to the evidence that much larger programs are economically feasible.[8] We believe that we can take this proposition as our point of departure. There are serious questions, of course (as noted in the preceding chapter), as to whether or not extremely large programs are politically feasible—whether or not United States consumers in the aggregate are ever willing to cut back on consumption. Even if reductions of consumption are ruled out, however, growth of the economy of the United States would by itself permit increases in defense outlays up to about $10 billion per year. If we wished to do so, therefore, we could raise the annual defense budget by $20 billion in two years' time without cutting aggregate consumption, investment, or civil government programs.[9] To repeat, then, the defense budget is not near any absolute upper limit.

On the other hand, there is no particular national security program that we need in an absolute sense. As mentioned in Chapter 2, a list of the "desirable" items that could strengthen our defense would be almost endless. Where does one draw the line (without reference to cost) between what is needed and what is not? There are no clear-cut "minimal" needs, either for defense as a whole or for particular programs. President Eisenhower has emphasized this point:

> Words like "essential" and "indispensable" and "absolute minimum" become the common coin of the realm—and they are spent with wild abandon. One military man will argue hotly for a given number of aircraft as the "absolute minimum." . . . And others will earnestly advocate the "indispensable" needs for ships or tanks or rockets or guided missiles or artillery—all totaled in numbers that are always called "minimum." All such views are argued with vigor and tenacity. But obviously all cannot be right.[10]

Outlays for various programs *can* be cut if we feel that we need other things even more. It is up to us to choose.

In brief, our national security budget is not near any physical limits—GNP minus subsistence, on the one hand, or zero expenditures, on the other. Also, because of growth, large *future* increases could be accomplished without cutting consumption. Consequently,

---

[8] On this subject, the writers agree with many of the general conclusions in the study by Gerhard Colm, *Can We Afford Additional Programs for National Security?*, National Planning Association, Washington, D.C., October 1953, and the subsequent paper by Gerhard Colm and Manuel Helzner, "General Economic Feasibility of National Security Programs," March 1957, published in *Federal Expenditure Policy for Economic Growth and Stability*, Hearings Before the Subcommittee on Fiscal Policy of the Joint Economic Committee, 85th Congress, 1st Session, U.S. Government Printing Office, Washington, D.C., 1958, pp. 356–364.

[9] The hypothetical programs discussed by Colm and Helzner, *op. cit.*, do not imply reductions in aggregate consumption.

[10] "The Eisenhower Tax Program," *U.S. News and World Report*, May 29, 1953, p. 98.

our range of choice is wide. Making the choice should be viewed as a problem of getting the most out of resources, not as one of hunting for a tablet on which the right budget, requirement, or doctrine is inscribed. In formulating defense budgets we should not be "need- or doctrine-firsters"—those who insist upon discovering what we "need" regardless of what we have to give up. Nor should we be "budget-firsters"—those who insist upon discovering what we can give up regardless of how much we value defense activities. Instead let us be deliberate choosers, changing our budgets and reshaping our forces as long as a change appears to gain more than it costs. If taken literally, the questions, "What can we afford for defense?" and "What are our needs?" are the wrong ones to ask in deciding upon the size of the defense effort. The right question is, "How much is needed for defense *more than it is needed for other purposes?*"

HOW MUCH FOR PROGRAMS VERSUS HOW MUCH FOR OBJECTS [11]

In trying to answer the above question, we should probably think in terms of programs—that is, combinations of activities that produce distinguishable products. A governmental program is the counterpart of an industry in the private sector of the economy— and is just as ambiguous, as hard to define, and yet as useful a concept as an industry. There is one important difference, however. In the private sector of the economy, markets reveal prices for industry outputs, even if they are intermediate products. In the governmental sector, there are no markets for most outputs, and the significance of the products, especially quantities of intermediate outputs, becomes especially hard to judge. To facilitate judgments about their value, programs should be aggregations of activities yielding products that can be at least subjectively appraised. In general, we should move toward thinking in terms of programs that perform tasks and yield end-products,[12] speaking rather loosely, rather than actions that yield objects or intermediate products.

Let us illustrate the distinction between a program and an object (we use this terminology because the *Budget of the United States* has made a similar distinction between "programs" and "objects"). Certain activities of the Air Force, the Army, and the

---

[11] For other discussions of some of these points and of related topics, see Arthur Smithies, especially pp. 229–277, and Jesse Burkhead, *Government Budgeting,* John Wiley and Sons, New York, 1956, pp. 110–181.

[12] David Novick, "Which Program Do We Mean in 'Program Budgeting'?" The RAND Corporation, P-530, May 12, 1954.

Navy produce retaliatory striking power or deterrence, and these activities might be grouped together and called a program. In providing deterrence, the Services use missiles, manpower, food, paper clips, and transportation—intermediate items which might be called "objects of expenditure."

Several points about programs and objects should be noted. First, decisions about the size of programs and those about the things to be bought are interdependent. One would not make one of these decisions in complete ignorance of the other. If the desired striking power is increased, different types of equipment may become the most efficient means, and if some equipment innovation appears (for example, more accurate ballistic missiles), a different level of striking power may become the proper choice. But to some extent these choices have to be made separately —by different people or at different times. In making one choice we try to make reasonable assumptions about the other.

Second, just what one means by an "end-product" or a "program" is not unambiguous. The line of demarcation between programs and objects is not clear-cut. Is the Military Air Transport Service a program or simply an activity supporting, say, the Tactical Air program? Or is even the latter merely something to be purchased for a program that might be called "deterrence and fighting of limited wars"? Even such tasks as providing nuclear striking power and providing forces for limited war have interrelationships. Neither is solely a supporting activity of the other, yet each can influence the credibility and effectiveness of the other. It may seem that one is driven to regard every military item and activity as an object purchased for and contributing to *one* program—national security.

Despite these complexities, officials do find it helpful to think in terms of several programs, and there is hope of developing categories that will be even more meaningful. After all, our only chance of pondering the gains as well as the costs of defense budgets is to think in terms of rather broad aggregations of activities. We cannot appraise the adequacy of the defense budget, either subjectively or with the aid of quantitative analysis, by thinking about the gains from such categories as paper clips, petroleum, or personnel. Nor can we go to the other extreme and think in terms of a single national security program. Such an aggregation is too broad; we have no conception of units of "national security" that could be purchased. But there are possibilities between these extremes—aggregations of activities that produce species of end-products such as capabilities for nuclear retaliation or for limited war. Complications and difficulties abound, and yet for some such programs we can make judgments about, or even develop quantitative clues to, their worth as well as their cost.

Perhaps an analogy from a consumer's budget will help clarify those points. An individual cannot judge intelligently how much he should spend on a car if he asks, "How much should I devote to fenders, to steering activities, and to carburetion?" Nor can he improve his decisions much by lumping all living into a single program and asking, "How much should I spend on life?" Yet it is often helpful to ask, "How much am I willing to spend on my car-program—on transportation to work, stores, and recreational facilities?" Although not really an end-item, an individual's transportation is closer to an end-product than fenders or carburetors. While his car program is somewhat interrelated with, say, his recreational program, the interrelationships do not dominate the outcome, and he can get some feeling for the gains from the car, making reasonable assumptions about the other program.

In determining the size of the defense budget, then, we should ask whether various broad programs should be increased or decreased, and we should keep trying to define programs about which we can make sounder judgments. To be sure, attention should also be given to detailed objects of expenditure. They help determine the efficiency with which the programs are carried out, and much of the economics of defense pertains to increasing the efficiency with which resources are employed *within* defense programs. The way the Services use materials and manpower deserves hard scrutiny—even at the highest levels. If Congress, through the review of defense expenditures, can perceive better ways to combine objects of expenditure or discover wasteful purchases that can be eliminated, it should certainly insist upon the increased efficiency.

But the objects of expenditure already get a goodly share of attention at the Congressional level. The annual hearings on appropriations are to a considerable extent about such matters as maintenance costs, the utilization of surplus butter and cheese by the Services, the location of National Guard armories, aircraft fuel and oil, travel costs, and the location of flag officers' quarters. Attention is attracted by things like the 104-year supply of Jeep parts once held by the Services or the 11,000 dozen oyster forks owned on one occasion by the Navy.[13] Here we wish to stress that

---

[13] Paul H. Douglas, *Economy in the National Government*, University of Chicago Press, Chicago, 1952, p. 150. To make matters worse, it turned out that "10,442 dozen of these oyster forks were of such a poor quality that, so the records showed, they were usable only in an emergency!"

the broader problem, the selection of the scale of defense programs, also deserves careful attention. At whatever degree of efficiency can be achieved, the question remains: Should the nation buy larger or smaller national-security programs? Are the last increments to existing programs worth this cost? Would further increments to particular programs be worth more than their cost?

HOW TO APPROACH THE CHOICE OF PROGRAM-SIZES [14]

To the preceding questions, we cannot provide definitive quantitative answers, of course. No analysis can yield solutions to the problem of choosing program-sizes that would necessarily be valid for all Congressmen and voters. Each person's answer depends upon how much value he attaches to deterrence of nuclear war, to the checking of limited aggressions, and to other products of national defense. It depends upon his attitude toward risks and uncertainty—that is, upon whether he is inclined to gamble or to hedge. It depends upon his valuation of side effects or impacts that cannot be made commensurable (in any *generally* valid way) with the main effects of the programs. Nevertheless, we can devise exhibits and analyses that facilitate weighing the gains and costs of alternative program-sizes. In deciding how much (if any) penicillin to buy, a man with pneumonia does not know precisely. how much he values good health, how to assess the risks, or precisely what the side effects will be; but it helps a lot to know how much penicillin costs and what effect it has on pneumonia.

It might be reemphasized that judgments or measurements of gains are just as important as measures of the costs (which are really the alternative gains that could be obtained if the resources were put to other uses). We cannot make intelligent decisions on the basis of either alone. In this section we turn first to exhibits of costs and then to the possibilities of appraising gains, in both instances taking the exhibits in recent budgets as points of departure. In doing this, we must regard certain changes, such as more extensive crossing of departmental lines, as being feasible. Crossing departmental boundaries could be achieved either by organizational changes or by the preparation of special exhibits separate from the main budget documents.

Breakdowns of Cost in Recent Budgets

Since 1949 the budgetary presentations in the Department of Defense have been improved. Proposed obligational authority and

---

[14] In various parts of this section the writers are indebted to David Novick of The RAND Corporation.

expenditures [15] have been collected into one document and put into somewhat more meaningful categories than had previously been used.[16] These recent compilations probably make possible more informed judgments about expenditure levels than could be made in earlier years. Nonetheless, the current presentation falls far short of being an effective program budget. Perhaps the best way to demonstrate this shortcoming is to present and discuss briefly a few sample exhibits from a recent budget.

The broad functional budget. To begin with, there is the broad functional budget in which all defense activities are put into one huge program called "major national security." [17] This is indeed an end-product program, but it is *too* comprehensive—embracing all Army, Navy, Air Force, and other national-security missions. To appreciate its cost and significance is almost impossible. Few persons have any subjective "feel" for a national-security capability—that is, for the output that would be provided. And there is little hope of ever devising quantitative measures that would shed much light on this mixture of capabilities. To try to sort out several less inclusive programs would seem to be a more promising approach.

The current "performance" budgets of the individual services. The present budget does classify expenditures into less inclusive categories that have been called programs. (In the Budget for the fiscal year 1960, they are often labeled "appropriation groups.") There are fairly detailed exhibits in terms of both programs and objects. The classification of expenditures by program, however, turns out to be a classification by organization unit (Army, Navy, or Air Force) and account title,[18] though the exhibits for each account title include a few paragraphs purporting to describe the program and its performance. Consider the summary presentation at the front of the section devoted to the Department of Defense.

---

[15] In the U.S. Budget, "obligational authority" is total authority to make commitments during the designated fiscal year, whether the cash is to be expended in that year or later on; and "expenditures" are the estimated disbursements during the fiscal year, whether the obligations were incurred in that year or previously. We shall refer mostly to obligational authority here, believing that it approximates future costs more closely than would the scheduled disbursements.

[16] For comments on the form of earlier budgets and the evolution of the current form, see Smithies, pp. 232–237.

[17] The other governmental functions are international affairs and finance, veterans' services and benefits, labor and welfare, agriculture and agricultural resources, natural resources, commerce and housing, general government, interest, and allowance for contingencies. *The Budget of the United States Government for the Fiscal Year Ending June 30, 1960*, U.S. Government Printing Office, Washington, D.C., 1959, p. M25.

[18] The "account titles" are the major "programs" listed in table 2.

In order to conserve space, Table 2 omits proposed expenditures and shows only proposed new obligations.[19]

Table 2.   Budget Authorizations and Expenditures[a] by Major Appropriation Groups or "Programs" (millions of dollars)

Appropriation groups[b]	New obligational authority		
	1958 enacted	1959 estimate	1960 estimate
Military personnel—total	10,982	11,475	11,625
Operation and maintenance	10,237	10,306	10,512
Procurement—total	11,054	14,524	13,348
Research, development, test, and evaluation	2,258	3,464	3,772
Construction—total	2,086	1,369	1,563
Revolving and management funds	130	—	30
Total, Department of Defense........	36,747	41,138	40,850

[a] Source: *The Budget of the United States Government for the Fiscal Year Ending June 30, 1960*, p. 445.

[b] Amounts for these "appropriation groups" are further subdivided into amounts for certain subgroups and for the branches of the Service (Army, Air Force, Navy), but the groups shown here are the basic categories that have been regarded as programs.

Note the nature of these "programs." Few of the items on this list are even remotely like end-product missions, and the dollar amounts are not the costs of achieving capabilities in such missions. Instead, the items are collections of objects used in a variety of tasks; and the dollar figures are the sums of selected costs from all of them. For instance, "military personnel" covers officers and men for all military functions. "Military personnel, Air Force" includes men for the Strategic Air Command, Tactical Air Command, and all other Air Force activities.

How does one choose the amount that should be spent on categories like across-the-board procurement or military personnel? Surely this choice is made by seeking the most efficient way of carrying out end-product programs such as achieving a nuclear deterrence force. And efficiency *within* programs can and should be sought more carefully than by pondering proposed expenditures for total personnel, procurement, and construction. Indeed, the use of these categories is likely to cause inefficiency. Procurement of new missiles or aircraft often has special glamor or appeal, and the Services may find that the best way to get money is to ask for increased procurement authority. Other categories such as military

---

[19] See footnote 15 for an explanation of these terms.

construction may appear to be relatively remote from operational capabilities and be neglected.[20] As a consequence, vital actions such as the dispersing and hardening of our deterrent force are postponed, and the constraints on specific objects of expenditure (like governmental allocations of specific materials to firms) bring about unbalanced inefficient operations. In short, this classification of expenditures by account titles gives little help either in choosing program levels or in seeking efficiency within programs.[21]

It was mentioned at the outset that current budgetary exhibits include breakdowns of expenditure both by programs (so-called) and by objects. To make clear what these objects are and why they do not convey useful information about end-product programs, Table 3 presents a sample breakdown of authorizations by objects —the one for Army personnel.

Table 3. Object Classification of Obligations for "Military Personnel, Army," 1960 Estimates[a]

Object Classification	Obligations in millions of dollars
01 Personal services: military	2,989
02 Travel	172
03 Transportation of things	49
07 Other contractual services	13
08 Supplies and materials	233
11 Grants, subsidies, and contributions	—
12 Pensions, annuities, and insurance claims	3
14 Interest	1
15 Taxes and assessments	55
Total direct obligations	3,514[b]

a Source: *The Budget of the United States Government for the Fiscal Year Ending June 30, 1960*, p. 460.

b The individual items do not add up to this total because of rounding. For "grants, subsidies, and contributions," the amount was less than $500,000.

The amounts proposed for these object classes (such as travel or transportation of things) may aid officials in locating in-

---

20 A tendency to neglect construction or other investments that do not yield a quick or tangible output is sometimes suggested by the communications underlying budgetary guidelines. For instance, one assumption used in a memorandum sent to the departmental secretaries in connection with the budget for fiscal year 1955 was as follows: "Military public works programs will be limited to those items for which there is an immediate operational requirement" (*Study of Airpower*, p. 1644).

21 The budget also contains a further breakdown of these so-called programs (classifications by account title) by "activities." For instance, obligations for Air Force Military Personnel are broken down into amounts for pay and allowances, subsistence in kind, and so on. These categories are again types of objects, and they help little in appraising program levels.

efficiencies; though systematic analysis would be necessary before anyone could be reasonably sure where inefficiency existed. Such a list of amounts can scarcely assist anyone, however, in weighing alternative program levels.

Improving the Breakdown of Costs

The first step in trying to improve our choice of program sizes is probably to put budget figures into categories that more nearly correspond to end-product missions.[22] Officials can make more perceptive judgments about the importance to the nation of these missions than they can make about the worth of categories like those listed above. Moreover, as will be indicated near the end of this chapter, there is hope of devising useful quantitative clues to the importance of end-product missions.[23] Thus, for these programs, there would be both rough estimates of the costs and a chance of gauging the gains.

A budget designed to show the approximate costs of such missions would naturally have to cross departmental lines. Activities that contribute to a broad military capability are seldom confined to one branch of the Service. Air Force activities, Naval operations, and the Army's role in active defense contribute to strategic deterrence, and all three departments also contribute to limited-war capability. The sort of exhibit that might be used to set over-all program levels is illustrated by Table 4. In this presentation, there would be essentially three broad programs: (1) deterrence or fighting of all-out war, (2) deterrence or fighting of limited war, and (3) research and development. Each of these would be divided into component missions. Many of the latter would be interdependent to a great degree (the broad programs to a lesser degree), and the costs of one would depend in part upon the sizes of the others. Some parts, such as a submarine force or a transport fleet, would contribute to both the nuclear deterrent capability and the limited-war mission.

In principle, one always likes to know the incremental or *extra* cost of whatever policy or program he is considering. If he considers two programs and a certain item is necessary for each of

---

[22] One format (using the Air Force as an example) has been suggested by G. H. Fisher in "Weapon-System Cost Analysis," *Operations Research*, October 1956, pp. 568–571.

Another "pro forma budget," also using the Air Force as an example, has been proposed in Smithies, pp. 265–277. In this format, major "programs" include forces in being, support of forces in being, force build-up, and mobilization reserves, with the first three broken down into strategic, tactical, air defense, and air transport portions.

[23] We use the term loosely. At best, as was pointed out earlier, no aggregation of defense activities yields an output that is unambiguously an independent end-product, and *some* "programs" will inevitably comprise leftovers or aggregations that are not very meaningful.

Table 4. Possible Format of National Security Budget

Programs and sub-programs	Proposed force composition (No. military units, where applicable)				Expenditures implied by proposed programs			
	'60	'61 ...	'64	'65	'60	'61 ...	'64	'65
Deterrence or Fighting of All-Out War								
Nuclear Striking Force (AF, Navy)								
B–47								
B–52								
Atlas								
Polaris								
.								
.								
etc.								
Active Defense (Army, Navy, AF)								
Early Warning								
Interceptors								
F–102								
Bomarc								
.								
.								
etc.								
Local Defense								
Nike								
.								
.								
etc.								
Passive Defense (OCDM)								
Dispersal								
Shelters, Evacuation								
Recuperation Planning								
Deterrence or Fighting of Limited Wars								
Ground Forces (Army, Marine)								
Sea Power (Navy)								
Tactical Air (AF, Navy)								
Transport, Air and Sea (AF, Navy)								
Military Aid to Other Countries (Mutual Security)								
Reserves for Mobilization								
Military Units (Army, Navy, AF)								
Defense Production (OCDM)								
Research and Development (AEC, AF, Army, Navy)								
Exploratory								
Weapon Systems								
General Administration								
Miscellaneous								

them, its cost cannot properly be allocated between the two. One can ask several different questions: whether Programs A + B are worth their combined cost (including any unallocable items), whether Program A is worth its incremental cost, or whether Program B is worth its incremental cost. Proper costing depends upon which of the questions is being asked. Since preparing and digesting numerous cost estimates is itself rather costly, however, it is uneconomic to insist on precise estimates. In the budgetary exhibits suggested here, the costs of programs and program-increments would be rough approximations. Joint costs might be allocated among programs according to crude rules of thumb, or sometimes assigned to one program with recognition that others were being aided. Some items used jointly, such as top administration, could be considered as a separate aggregate (called, for the sake of convenience, a program).

These particular aggregations simply represent one set of possibilities. There may be others that would be equally or more useful. It might be better if exploratory development and weapon systems development were explicitly regarded as separate programs, their proposed costs never being lumped together into a single figure. Additional programs might be formulated from the activities in the "all other" or "miscellaneous" category. In a general way, however, Table 4 does indicate the way we should approach the choice of program-sizes and the direction in which our budgetary exhibits should probably be evolving.[24]

Notice that this format would project the costs entailed by these programs, year by year, for several years ahead. This information (for example, about future operating costs, which are sometimes extremely heavy) is essential in making decisions about program levels.[25] Yet conventional budgetary documents do not reveal the future expenditures that are implied by proposed programs. Future expenditures are vitally important whether the new programs are larger or smaller, that is, whether our concern is with initiating new programs or with terminating old ones. For frequently the major impact of either will be felt not in the next year, but in

---

[24] The use of the suggested exhibits would call for, or be aided by, a number of changes in current estimation procedures—for example, increased emphasis on the use of statistical cost factors and a shortened budget cycle, increased attention to costs *during* the formulation of proposed programs (i.e., prior to their translation into budgets), improved cost analysis, and perhaps a better system of accrual accounting. Some of these reforms are discussed in Smithies, pp. 237–265, and in David Novick, "Weapon-System Cost Methodology," The RAND Corporation, Report R–287, February 1, 1956. See also Fisher, pp. 558–571.

[25] Note, however, that only costs which are genuinely entailed should be so shown. R and D programs, for instance, do *not* imply the procurement and operation of the whole menu of weapon systems that are under development.

the more distant future. Expenditures in the first year on a new weapon system, for example, are likely to be a small proportion of the ultimate future cost of procurement and operation. Similarly, the savings from canceling a going program are often mainly or exclusively in future years: in the current budgetary year the costs of cancellation may equal or even exceed any gross savings. The flexibility in the budget in any current year, in either direction, is small compared with the possible impact of program decisions this year on the budgets of future years. The fact that everyone is mainly concerned with the current annual budget is frustrating because that budget has so little "give," and inefficient, because it neglects the larger, hidden part of the budget iceberg.

Actually, what is needed is an exhibit similar to table 4 for each of several program levels. Then the Administration and the Congress could choose among explicit, meaningful programs in deciding upon the size of the defense budget.[26] When only one program level is presented, either additions to the budget or cuts in it must be made blindly—and sometimes with consequences that are worse than they need be. Disproportionate cuts may be made in some budget categories, or supplements may be voted to others which will buy little in the way of military capability without corresponding increases in complementary activities. Adjustment may require frantic and inefficient reprogramming. With a range of alternative levels prepared in advance, adjustments could be made by simply turning to a level that had been consciously considered and whose elements had been balanced.

Charles Silberman and Sanford Parker, in an article entitled "The Economic Impact of Defense," [27] attempted in 1958 to calculate the costs of, and indicate the gains from, alternative supplementary defense programs proposed by the Rockefeller Brothers Fund Report,[28] the official Gaither Report,[29] and others. They conclude on costs: "The Administration's defense program now calls for a rise from $43.3 billion in fiscal 1958 to $45.5 billion in fiscal 1959, with the rate of increase slowing down thereafter. The Rockefeller program would have spending rise to $53.2 billion in fiscal 1961, while the third program, as *Fortune* has called it—a synthesis of the recommendations of experts who worked on the Gaither Report and other studies—would have spending rise to $65

---

[26] Of course, where possible, the indicators of performance discussed below should also be estimated and presented for each of the alternative budget levels.

[27] *Fortune* Magazine, June 1958, p. 102.

[28] *International Security—The Military Aspect*, published by the Rockefeller Brothers Fund, Inc., 1958.

[29] As reported in unconfirmed press stories. The Report itself has not been made public.

billion in fiscal 1963. And still other experts urge programs that would add up to perhaps $75 billion." Unfortunately the Congress and the public must make up their minds about the right size of defense budget with little official information of this sort about the costs or gains of either larger or smaller programs.

Indicators of Performance in Recent Budgets

The next step toward improving our decisions about program-sizes is to get better information about the outputs of alternative programs. Budgetary presentations today do attempt to describe the product that is being purchased. At the beginning of the portion of the United States Budget pertaining to the Department of Defense, there is an informative discussion of force structure and of certain military activities.

Moreover, since 1949, when the Services were instructed to submit "performance budgets," they have classified proposed outlays into the so-called programs that were previously discussed, and have tried to indicate the output or performance that would be purchased. These indicators are not very revealing, however, chiefly because the categories into which outlays are grouped are remote from end-product programs. As an example, consider the paragraphs on the performance of the "military personnel" category—one of the programs mentioned earlier in connection with table 2.

MILITARY PERSONNEL [30]

The following narrative statement covers the active duty appropriations for the Army, Navy, Marine Corps, and Air Force.

1. *Pay and allowances.*—This provides for the pay and allowances of military personnel on active duty including cadets and midshipmen at the three service academies, aviation cadets, and other officer candidates.

The number of active duty military personnel provided for is shown in the following table. The personnel in the civilian components of the Defense forces are described under the pertinent appropriations below.

In addition, provision is made for payment for proficiency advancements to selected enlisted personnel in critical-skill areas. Funds are provided for advancement of 80,000 men by June 30, 1959, and 163,000 men by June 30, 1960. It also provides for the Government's contribution to the Federal old-age and survivors insurance trust fund under the Servicemen's and Veterans' Survivor Benefits Act, purchase of individual clothing for initial issue to enlisted personnel, replacement of clothing issues in Korea, and for payment of clothing maintenance allowances.

---

[30] This excerpt from the narrative statement (in budgets prior to that for fiscal-year 1960, it was entitled "Program and Performance") is from *The Budget of the United States Government for the Fiscal Year Ending June 30, 1960*, p. 459. In the published statement the exhibit includes the "average number" as well as the "year-end number" of personnel.

2. *Subsistence in kind.*—This provides for the purchase of food supplies for issue as rations to enlisted personnel including emergency and operational rations.

3. *Movements, permanent change of station.*—This provides for. . . .

		Year-end Number	
		Estimate	
	Actual 1958	1959	1960
Defense total	2,599,848	2,525,000	2,520,000
Officers	325,460	318,515	316,045
Enlisted	2,264,290	2,194,091	2,190,911
Officer candidates	10,098	12,394	13,044
Army	898,192	870,000	870,000
Officers	104,220	100,100	100,100
Enlisted	792,271	768,200	768,200
Military Academy cadets	1,701	1,700	1,700

The only parts of the above passage that convey much information are the numbers, and, since personnel are ingredients rather than end-products, even they are not very helpful. Sometimes, descriptions of performance are a good deal worse, constituting merely lyrical pleas for a program. The following example, though it pertains to nondefense (and non-Federal) activities, illustrates the generalities that are sometimes used to describe performance:

> Instead of thinking of money alone . . . citizens should hear children singing in the spring concert, travel with the crippled child in early morning from his home to his special unit, feel that school roofs are tight and walls are safe, see the pupils in the corridors washing their dirty hands and drying their clean ones, accompany in spirit the injured child to the hospital for treatment, and see salmon fishing in Alaska with children in the fifth grade. A top performance budget paints pictures in words that justify the expenditure.[31]

Small wonder that some officials (for example, Mr. John Taber, long of the House Appropriations Committee) prefer a budget in terms of objects to be purchased. (With the latter one can at least try to say something about the internal efficiency of programs.) The advantages of a program budget are considerably reduced if

---

[31] Harold E. Akerly, "For Better Public Relations Use a Performance Budget," *Nation's Schools*, February 1951, p. 37, copyright 1951, The Modern Hospital Publishing Co., Chicago; all rights reserved; cited in Jesse Burkhead, *Government Budgeting*, John Wiley and Sons, Inc., New York, 1956, p. 138.

the indicators of performance are uninformative or downright misleading.

IMPROVING THE INDICATORS OF PERFORMANCE

If activities are grouped into more meaningful missions, however, it seems likely that better subjective appraisals of output can be made and also that better indicators of performance can be provided. There is no hope, of course, of measuring the ultimate "worth" of defense. It is obviously impossible to put a generally valid price tag on the output. The gains from program increments cannot therefore be expressed in the same units as the costs, and the two cannot be compared in terms of a common denominator. But there is hope of describing the product meaningfully, and some ways of describing it are more meaningful than others. Similarly, no researcher can measure the ultimate worth of a new car to a particular consumer. But there is hope of meaningfully describing this product, and what the car will do is a more meaningful description to the consumer than the car's chemical composition.

Changes in force structure. As a first approximation, force structure for each category in Table 4—numbers of B–52 wings, Atlas squadrons, army and naval units of various types—would be much closer to the end-products than the numbers of personnel or pieces of equipment. To some extent, the quantity of wings and divisions in each category suggests what is being purchased. Note that this information is constantly used at present. Officials in the Services and in the Defense Department are as familiar with force structure as they are with their own names. Part of the information is published in the Budget and is fully aired in Congressional hearings on appropriations. Even so, force structure may not be considered systematically *in conjunction with costs* as in Table 4, for costs by such military units have seldom been presented. Long-range planning and also programming have been in terms of military units, but budgeting (that is, translating the programs into costs) has usually been in terms of other categories.

Numbers of wings and divisions, however, do not reveal enough about capabilities. For one thing, force structure per se may not tell much about the kind of capability that it provides. An augmentation of our forces may increase our capability to strike first, but not our ability to strike second. If so, it may help deter minor aggressions somewhat, but as far as the thermonuclear war is concerned, it may produce negative deterrence. Or, additional divisions may increase our ability to fight World War II but not our strength in more likely kinds of conflict. If so, they may produce small gains.

The enemy's response. For another thing, force structure per se does not tell us anything about the enemy's position or about his probable reaction to changes in the structure of our forces. Yet what our forces buy for us is clearly relative to the enemy's capability and his reaction to our decisions. This fact can hardly be emphasized enough. The pertinent question is whether or not we are buying sufficient strength, *relative to potential enemy forces* (when fairly sensible strategies are attributed to him), to deter central war and cope with limited aggressions. We need a higher national security budget if the potential enemy is Soviet Russia than if it is Argentina; higher if we have no allies than if we have reliable ones; higher if the enemy devotes 20 per cent of his national product to the military efficiently than if he devotes 10 per cent inefficiently; higher if the enemy increases his technological and industrial capability in future relative to ours, while devoting the same proportion to military purposes; higher if our strategy draws containment lines in the Eastern Hemisphere than if these are drawn at our own shores. Discussion of the appropriate size of military budgets often misses this essential point of relativity. An increase in the absolute efficiency with which we use resources ("more bang for a buck") creates no presumption that the budget can be cut when a potential enemy is correspondingly increasing his absolute efficiency ("more rubble for a ruble").

Thus when considering program increments or decrements, we must try to take into account the enemy's position and probable response. Are our forces strong enough, and properly designed, in view of his situation and his capabilities? If we add to our forces in a particular way, can he easily counter our move? What deterrent capability (or ability to fight local wars and keep them limited) will we end up with? Will our action yield a better basis for finding mutually advantageous weapon limitations or disarmament measures?

For these several reasons, most simple indicators of performance, including changes in force structure, that would be affected by program increments or decrements are not sufficiently revealing. Fortunately, it is often possible to indicate in more significant terms what program increments will buy.

Changes in designated capabilities. It is possible to make analyses comparing alternative ways of carrying out broad missions such as the strategic deterrence mission. Such analyses seek to answer questions like: Which combination of means yields the greatest deterrent capability for a given budget? Capability may be measured by the destruction that could be inflicted on potential enemies in selected (and not improbable) contingencies even if we received the first strike. Part III will deal with the methods and possibilities of comparing various courses of action in planning defense. Here we wish only to point out that similar analyses can be devised to answer a different type of question: What capabilities are yielded by different program levels? What change in capability result from program increments or decrements? The analyses would by no means point to the preferred program level —but they would give highly relevant indicators of performance.

Analysis could also provide revealing indicators of another gain from portions of the strategic deterrence mission—namely the contribution of retaliatory capability, active defenses, passive defenses, and recuperation planning to the chance of survival in the event of enemy attack. Analysis could give a rough yet informative picture of, say, capital, human beings, and emergency stocks that would survive a plausible enemy attack. These data, in conjunction with program costs, would also help in choosing among alternative program levels.

In addition, analysis of this sort might be able to reveal what different program-levels could accomplish in the limited-war mission (another of the broad programs listed in table 4). Calculations might give clues to the scale and kinds of local aggressions that could be "handled" with alternative programs for limited-war capability. The results would constitute quantitative clues to what we could do in various plausible contingencies. Obviously the outcomes of such conflicts could not be projected with precision. Nonetheless, such clues to our capability would be more revealing than numbers of divisions, tactical air units, and so on.

These indicators of gain would not embrace all possible effects of program changes. There would be spillover effects on other programs. For instance, a change in strategic deterrence capability would have some influence on our prospects regarding limited conflicts. There would also be other impacts not reflected in the suggested indicators of performance—impacts on our relations with neutral or friendly nations, on the basis for trying to reach mutually advantageous agreements with enemy nations, and so on. There would be further indirect effects on our economy. But a budget in terms of broad programs for which such indicators of performance could be provided would help sort out the major implications of alternative budgets. It would facilitate the task of weighing the costs and gains of budget increments or decrements.

As for the research and development program, there is probably no good way of indicating the performance that would be purchased with alternative program-levels. Research and development activities are by nature explorations into an unknown and distant future. Estimating the results of research is even more uncertain than measuring the consequences of, say, future programs for limited war. We can try to estimate the potential gains *if* certain break-throughs or developments can be achieved, and such estimates are valuable clues in shaping research and development programs. Even though estimates of potential payoff are helpful, however, tremendous uncertainties must be recognized. Exploratory research and development often produces quite unpredicted payoffs. Hence, while the output of research and development is of enormous significance to future capabilities, that output is extremely uncertain in both form and magnitude, and there is no way to show what a particular year's program will produce. Judgment on the size and character of the program must be based largely on experience with similar programs in the past, taking both failures and successes into account.

It is partly for this reason that it seems to be appropriate to segregate research and development as a separate program or programs. In a sense it is a supporting activity. But we do not know to what extent it will turn out to support strategic deterrence and to what extent it will support other missions. Moreover, because the program's objective is to acquire knowledge rather than to carry out a well-defined task, research and development should be managed differently from operational missions. It is best, therefore, to regard research and development as a separate program—probably to regard exploratory research and development and what might be called weapon-systems development as separate and distinct programs. But no over-all indicator of performance in these activities (or in Administration and Miscellaneous!) can be provided.

Where meaningful indicators are feasible, they would have to be separate presentations, not just a few numbers in another column of Table 4. But they would be introduced *along with* the breakdown of costs by broad missions. Like that breakdown of costs, the indicators of performance and the underlying analyses would usually have to bear a military classification. These tools could nonetheless be valuable to military planners, to officials in the Department of Defense and the Budget Bureau, and to Congressional leaders.

One aspect of the gains—and costs, for that matter—that merits a final mention is their uncertainty (a subject which will be considered in some detail in chapter VII). When a program increment is considered, one cannot see a particular outcome that is certain and that determines a unique set of gains. What one foresees is a number of potential outcomes, some more likely and others less likely, but all of them quite possible. This uncertainty makes the task of weighing gains and costs still more formidable. Instead of the question being, "What is the worth of this particular increase in capability?" the question is, "What is the worth of this probability distribution of increases in capability (or of this uncertain increase in capability)?" Furthermore, since steps can often be taken to hedge against contingencies, another question arises: "What is the worth of particular attempts to reduce uncertainty?"

Obviously, these questions are hard to answer. Different individuals, given the same information about prospective gains and costs, will answer differently. The main reason is that the answer depends upon one's attitude toward risk. Some people prefer a comparatively safe policy and will give up a great deal in order to reduce the chance of disaster. Others are willing to live more dangerously.

HOW BIG A BUDGET DURING HOT WAR?

If and when local conflicts break out, certain programs are likely to seem more important to us than had previously been the case. If the conflict lasts long, it will be imperative to expand certain activities. Consequently the national-security budget is almost certain to rise. The nature of the problem, however, is still the same. In order to decide how much should be spent on national security, one should think, not just about expenditures for objects, but about the gains and costs of having higher (or lower) programs. The types of gain and cost to be considered, and the analyses that would help one weigh them, are the same.

If all-out war involving unlimited objectives should occur, the choice among alternative budget *levels* would probably not concern us greatly. In the unlikely event that atomic weapons were not exchanged, the war would be similar in many respects to World War II. The budget would probably approach its upper limit— GNP minus subsistence and "necessary" supporting activities.[32] During the first few years of such a war, physical constraints (the difficulty of shifting resources from one activity to another) rather than budgetary ones might limit the diversion of resources to de-

---

[32] As explained earlier, it is difficult to determine such an upper limit, because it is hard to define "necessities." Someone always insists (quite properly): "Give me the luxuries of life, and I'll do without the necessities." But we can say that at some budget level, the sacrifice entailed by trying to devote more to defense becomes enormous.

fense. In any event, the considerations discussed above would probably not play much of a role in setting budget levels.

In the more likely event that unlimited war led to a thermonuclear exchange, interest in budget formulation would fall off considerably! In those circumstances, it would make little difference whether one thought in terms of programs or of objects; and the exhibits suggested above would have little bearing on the challenging problems of the day.

PART THREE

EFFICIENCY IN USING DEFENSE RESOURCES

V

EFFICIENCY IN MILITARY DECISIONS[1]

In this part we will assume that the amount of the nation's resources to be devoted to military use has been determined. Our problem is: How can we use these resources efficiently to buy military power, or more broadly, national security? Actually, the solutions to the problems of parts II and III are interdependent to some extent, and, as noted earlier, analyses of the sort to be described in part III are important in appraising the effectiveness of defense programs and therefore in deciding upon their size. However, we must usually tackle these choices—the size of the budget and the effective use of that budget—one at a time, making reasonable assumptions about one choice while analyzing the other.

While the efficient allocation or use of resources has always been the core problem of economic theory, economists have until recently made little attempt to apply the theory to military, or indeed any governmental, expenditure. A possible explanation is the small proportion of national resources formerly devoted to the military sector (indeed to the whole government) in the United States and other Western countries except in wartime. Now with the prospect of United States national security expenditure continuing indefinitely at 10 per cent or more of GNP and total government expenditure (including state and local) at two to three times this level,[2] the efficient use of the very large resources involved has become a matter of primary importance.

---

[1] Also pertinent are the articles in "Economics and Operations Research: A Symposium," *Review of Economics and Statistics*, August 1958, pp. 195–229.

[2] A great deal of what is said in this Part about the efficient use of resources by the military applies equally to many other kinds of government expenditure.

The reason the efficient use of military (and other government) resources is a special problem is the absence of any built-in mechanisms, like those in the private sector of the economy, which lead to greater efficiency. There is within government neither a price mechanism which points the way to greater efficiency, nor competitive forces which induce government units to carry out each function at minimum cost. Because of the lure of profits and the threat of bankruptcy, private firms are under pressure to seek out profitable innovations and efficient methods. In this search they have often used, and are now using to an increasing extent, formal quantitative analysis. But even if they do not, continued progress and increased efficiency still tend to come about, though less rapidly. After all, *some* firm is likely to discover more efficient methods through trial and error even in the absence of systematic analysis. Subsequently, other firms observing the resulting profits copy the innovation; those that fail to do so (that is, those who make inferior choices of methods) begin to suffer losses, and hence tend to be eliminated by the process of "natural selection." [3]

In government, by contrast, there is no profit lure, and promotions or salary increases do not depend on profits. In most operations, an objective criterion of efficiency is not readily available, and even if it were, incentives to seek profitable innovations and efficient (least cost) methods are not strong. There is scope for "Parkinson's law," [4] personal idiosyncrasy, and uneconomic preferences of officials to take hold, because the costs of choosing inefficient policies do not impinge upon the choosers. [5]

Finally, the process of natural selection, whose working depends upon the degree and type of rivalry, operates only weakly, if at all, to eliminate wasteful governments or government departments. The federal government, for instance, competes only with the political party that is out of office, and survival in this competition depends upon many factors other than efficiency in the use of resources. Thus, there is neither an adequate price mechanism to reveal the cheapest methods of performing public functions nor

---

[3] A. Alchian, "Uncertainty, Evolution, and Economic Theory," *The Journal of Political Economy,* LVIII, June 1950, pp. 211–221. The prevention of mistakes by systematic analysis would be a cheaper path to progress than their correction by natural selection—*if* the analyses always led to correct policies. On the difficulties of correct analysis we will have much to say below.

[4] C. Northcote Parkinson, *Parkinson's Law: and Other Studies in Administration,* Houghton Mifflin Co., Boston, 1957.

[5] For a provocative discussion of this matter, see the paper by A. Alchian and R. Kessel presented at the Universities-National Bureau of Economics Research Conference on Labor Economics in April, 1960.

any force which induces or compels the government to adopt such methods.[6]

THREE GENERAL APPROACHES

What, in these circumstances, can be done? We want efficiency; we want to obtain the greatest possible security from a given budget, both because national security is itself of such transcendent importance, and because the more efficient the use of the military budget the more resources we can have for nonmilitary purposes. But how, in a sector containing 10 per cent of the economy (much more if we include civilian government functions) with no adequate price mechanism and no institutions forcing natural selection of the efficient, can we achieve efficiency?

There are three possible approaches, interrelated and interdependent, which will be considered in this part of the book.

1. The improvement of institutional arrangements within the government to promote efficiency. Extreme proposals have been made which would simulate price and market mechanisms within the government. Less ambitious proposals would improve budgeting and accounting methods (see Chapter 4), attempt to provide more appropriate incentives, and reorganize the apparatus of decision making.
2. Increased reliance on systematic quantitative analysis to determine the most efficient alternative allocations and methods.
3. Increased recognition and awareness that military decisions, whether they specifically involve budgetary allocations or not, are in one of their important aspects economic decisions; and that unless the right questions are asked, the appropriate alternatives selected for comparison, and an economic criterion used for choosing the most efficient, military power and national security will suffer.

It is our conviction that something can be accomplished by the third approach alone—that is, by improved understanding of the nature of the problem—even without greater use of systematic quantitative analysis and with no changes in governmental structure. In formulating policy it does help to ask the right questions instead of the wrong ones. If the alternatives are arrayed, and a serious attempt made to apply sound criteria in choosing the most efficient ones, decisions are likely to be improved even though the

---

[6] In a few government activities, e.g., the Military Sea Transportation Service, simulation of the market mechanism is attempted.

considerations brought to bear are mainly qualitative and intuitive. There are enough responsible and highly motivated persons involved in the decision-making process—officers, civil servants, members of the Cabinet, Congressmen, and influential citizens—to make education in principles worthwhile for its own sake.

What may be even more important, as we shall see, is that any real improvement in the methods of quantitative analysis or in government structure to achieve economy is absolutely dependent upon a firm grasp of these principles. Quantitative analyses that are addressed to the wrong question or administrative devices that promote the wrong kind of economizing can easily do more harm than good.

The role of systematic quantitative analysis in military decisions is potentially much more important than in the private sector of the economy. It is obviously more important than in households because the problems are typically so much more complex. We all know families that manage well on their incomes, and families that manage poorly, apparently attaining a lower standard of life or running into recurrent financial difficulties despite apparently adequate incomes. Some of the good family managers may rely heavily on systematic quantitative analysis—on elaborate budget calculations, the studies of consumers' research organizations, and so on. But others do not, and in general we find little correlation between goodness of household management and reliance on systematic quantitative analysis. The overwhelmingly important factors are a firm grasp of principles and good sense or judgment. The quantitative relations are usually familiar, and simple enough for a man or woman of average intelligence to work out intuitively or in the margin of an account book.

In many military problems, however, this is not true. The quantitative relations may involve many different fields of technology as well as operational factors, and are sometimes so intricate that elaborate computations are necessary. There is almost never anyone who has an intuitive grasp of all the fields of knowledge that are relevant. For example, if we are comparing the relative merits of a high performance fighter and a cheaper fighter with somewhat lower performance, it is easy to see, qualitatively, that the more expensive aircraft will do better in a two-plane duel, but that we can have more aircraft on a billion dollar budget and thereby more interceptions and duels if we choose the plane with lower unit cost. But the problem is essentially quantitative, and depends upon fairly precise answers being developed to three questions: *How many* more of the cheaper plane can be procured and maintained on a billion dollar budget? What are the relative values of numbers and various performance characteristics in interception? *How much* better is the high performance plane in a duel? In some special cases we may be able to assemble a group of "experts," each of whom has a good intuitive grasp of the factors relevant for answering one of these subquestions, and after discussion emerge with a fairly unequivocal answer. But in general, and especially where, as is usually the case, the choice is not between two but among many, systematic quantitative analysis will help—or prove essential.

For a somewhat different reason systematic quantitative analysis is more important in military than in private business decisions. There is, as we have seen, an alternative process for achieving efficiency in private business—competition and natural selection—which would be fairly effective even if the variations in techniques were random. In government this alternative does not exist. Efficient techniques and policies have to be selected consciously; and wherever the relevant factors are diverse and complex, as they frequently are, unaided intuition is incapable of weighing them and making an efficient decision.

Sound analyses, it might be noted, can not only help identify efficient courses of action but can also improve incentives. The existence of good analyses cannot alter penalties and rewards so that "what is good for the chief of each department is also good for national security"; but their existence, in conjunction with rivalry between departments, may increase the cost to decision-makers of making uneconomic decisions. That is, the existence of sound analyses plus rival branches or departments that may make use of the arguments to get their budgets increased can cause each department to veer toward more efficient policies.

The possible utility of improved institutional arrangements for promoting the efficient use of resources by government departments has been the subject of much debate. This has in the past been the province, perhaps too exclusively, of the management efficiency experts. As economists we will not have much to say about government organization and structure. We believe, however, that what we say about criteria and methods of analysis can help in judging the efficacy of alternative organizational forms and that the development of practical institutions which encourage efficiency deserves far more attention than we or other economists have yet given it. It should at least be possible to remove some of the perverse incentives injected by such factors as special constraints, the premium placed on getting budgets raised rather than using budgets more efficiently, and cost-plus-fixed-fee contracts. There must be some way to provide postmasters and depot managers with more appropriate motivations, as well as to improve the government's decision-making machinery.

OPTIMAL, EFFICIENT, AND FEASIBLE POSITIONS

We have so far used the term "efficient" in a vague and general sense to mean "making good use" (including "making the best use") of available resources. Much of the time, though, we have in mind a more precise meaning for this term. We can best define it by contrasting "efficient," "optimal," and "feasible" positions.

In order to reach an *optimal* solution to problems of choice, we must be able to value various "situations" or outputs. Then we can revise our choices and shift resources to get the maximum value that is possible in the face of whatever constraints confront us. Even if we cannot always compare the values of different outputs, however, we can find some positions that yield more of some valuable outputs without yielding less of any others. When we cannot produce more of one output without sacrificing another, we have reached an *efficient* position. Many other situations are *feasible*, of course, by using the resources inefficiently. The differences between efficient positions and the others will be clearer if we consider a simple example.

ONE INPUT, TWO OUTPUTS

Suppose that we are concerned with the allocation of a military budget, fixed at $B billion, between the procurement (and maintenance in a state of readiness) of two forces—say, a strategic bombing force and an air defense force. Suppose further, for the sake of simplicity in this example, that the effectiveness of the strategic bombing force can be measured by a single number—the expected number of enemy targets that it could destroy after D Day—and that the effectiveness of the air defense force can be similarly measured by its "kill potential"—the number of attacking enemy bombers it could be expected to shoot down in certain circumstances.

We can draw a production-possibility curve, as in Figure 2, representing all possible *maximum* combinations of target destruction and kill potential which we can buy with $B billion—maximum in the sense that the fraction of the budget allocated to the strategic bombing force is spent in such a way as to maximize the target destruction potential of the force, and the fraction allo-

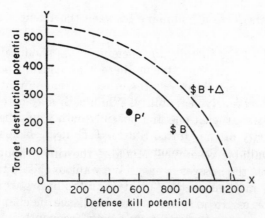

Figure 2. Production-possibility curve.

cated to air defense is so spent as to maximize kill potential.[7] The Y intercept represents the target destruction potential that we could achieve by spending all $B billions on the strategic air force, the X intercept the kill potential from spending all on air defense.

An efficient use of resources, in the technical sense, is one which makes it impossible to increase one valuable output without increasing a valuable input or decreasing another valuable output. It is apparent that each point on our curve represents an efficient use of resources in this sense; the curve is therefore a locus of "efficient points." At any point on the curve it is possible to increase target destruction only by moving to the left along the curve; that is, by decreasing kill potential, or by moving to a higher curve (dotted in fig. 2) representing a larger budget ($B + △ billion).

All points such as P' lying below and to the left of the curve of efficient points represent inefficient uses of resources, and are therefore called "inefficient points." They do, however, represent *feasible* uses of a budget of $B billion. We can draw up a plan to spend $B billion inefficiently to achieve a target destruction potential of only 200 and an air defense kill potential of only 500— probably all too easily. But if we did have such a plan, we could revise it, without additional budget, to increase target destruction potential without decreasing kill potential (or vice versa). We can always find several efficient points which are unequivocally superior to an inefficient point.

Note that the points lying above and to the right of the curve on Figure 2 are simply *infeasible* on a budget of $B billion. The

---

[7] The estimation of the points on this curve is, of course, the job of systematic quantitative analysis. The curves in this chapter are purely hypothetical.

efficient points form a boundary between the feasible and the infeasible points.

But which of the infinity of efficient points should our military planners choose? At one extreme there is an efficient point providing no offensive capability, at the other extreme an efficient point providing no defensive capability. While both may be efficient in a technical sense, at least one and possibly both would be disastrous for the security of the United States. Technical efficiency is not a sufficient condition for economic choice.

In principle the answer is easy: We want to choose that efficient point which maximizes the "utility" or "military worth" of the combined forces. In practice, as we shall see in chapter VI, the explicit measurement of military worth frequently presents formidable difficulties. If we abstract from these difficulties for the moment in order to clarify definitions, we can draw curves (called indifference curves) that reflect our preference for some combinations of target destruction and kill potential over others (fig. 3). Combinations represented on a curve to the right and higher (more of both goods) are obviously preferred to combinations on a curve to the left and lower (less of both). We are indifferent among com-

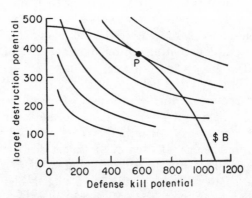

Figure 3.   Indifference curves and optimal point.

binations represented by different points on any single curve; we are willing to sacrifice some defense potential if we can obtain thereby a sufficiently enhanced offensive potential, and vice versa. Indifference curves are typically convex to the origin, which means that the more of one good (for example, offense) we give up, the less willing we are to sacrifice still more, and therefore the larger the increment of the other (for example, defense) we insist upon having in compensation.[8]

The *optimal* use of our $B billion budget is represented by the point of tangency of the original curve of figure 2 with an indifference curve (Point P, fig 3). From this point it is not possible to improve our position (that is, move to a higher indifference curve representing a preferred combination) by any change in allocation or use of resources.

If all portions of the production-possibility curve are not concave to the origin, there may be complications. The shape of this curve depends upon whether the costs of producing the goods measured on the axes are increasing or decreasing. Or, to put the matter another way, the shape depends upon whether the returns per extra dollar expended on the outputs are decreasing or increasing. Returns can usually be assumed to be decreasing, making the production-possibility curve concave to the origin. But there are troublesome counter-examples; for example, returns in terms of defense kill potential might be increasing if we consider extra outlays on plugging gaps in an almost completed radar line.[9] If there are increasing returns and part of the curve has a peculiar shape, we have to look at large reallocations as well as small ones.[10] We may find more than one point of tangency between the production-possibility curve and the indifference curves, or we may find no point of tangency and the highest indifference curve may be attained where the production-possibility curve intercepts one of the axes (that is, it may then be best to spend the entire budget on the item that yields increasing returns).

The frequent difficulty in locating *the* optimal point by systematic quantitative analysis, while unfortunate, should not be regarded as disastrous in all or even most practical problems of military choice. In the first place, decision-makers or their advisers who have thought deeply about a problem are likely to have shrewd ideas about the sector of the curve containing the optimal point, even if they cannot provide a mathematical proof of its exact location. If systematic quantitative analysis can narrow the choice

---

[8] The incremental amount of Y we need to compensate for an incremental loss of X is the slope of the indifference curve at any point. It is the rate at which we are willing to trade one for the other.

[9] Many plausible examples of "increasing returns," however, are really examples of rectifying errors, which can be done by redesigning one's proposal, not solely by expanding outlays along one axis or the other. If I forget to include a bathroom in my plans for a new house, and therefore the addition of a bathroom has a high payoff, is it correct to say that house construction is an example of increasing returns?

[10] Malcolm W. Hoag, "Some Complexities in Military Planning," *World Politics*, July 1959, pp. 553–576.

to a set of efficient points, the burden placed upon intuitive judgment is reduced and the quality of judgment should be improved. Secondly, optima are characteristically flat, like the crest of Half Dome rather than the peak of the Matterhorn. It isn't usually important to find the precise peak or point of tangency. On Figure 3 one can move along the opportunity curve for some distance on either side of the point of tangency without getting far from the highest attainable indifference curve.

In the third place, *the best practical aim of systematic quantitative analysis is to demonstrate that some course of action A is better than some alternative course of action B,* when B is what is proposed, or planned, or will otherwise occur. If B is an inefficient point, systematic quantitative analysis can find several efficient points A, A', A'', . . . which can be shown to be superior to B even if nothing is known about military worth except that certain capabilities, like target destruction and air defense kill potential, contribute to it (see fig. 4).

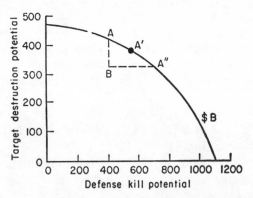

Figure 4. Efficient points versus inefficient points.

Let us emphasize once more that this concept of seeking efficient points is extremely important. For while we cannot usually find optimal, or second-best, or even *j*th-best, solutions, it frequently enables us to identify improvements over existing or proposed policies.[11]

---

[11] The difficulties of determining second-best policies have received some well-deserved attention in recent years. See I. M. D. Little, *A Critique of Welfare Economics,* Clarendon Press, Oxford, 1950, especially Chapter VII, pp. 110-120, and Chapter XV, pp. 267–272; J. E. Meade, *The Theory of International Economic Policy,* Vol. II, *Trade and Welfare,* Oxford University Press, London, 1955, Chapter VII, "The Marginal Conditions for the Second-Best," pp. 102–118; R. G. Lipsey and K. Lancaster, "The General Theory of Second Best," *Review of Economic Studies,* 1956–57, pp. 11–32; and M. J. Farrell, "In Defense of Public-Utility Price Theory," *Oxford Economic Papers,* February 1958, pp. 109–123.

TWO INPUTS, ONE OUTPUT

In the preceding example we considered a planning problem that involved the allocation of a single valuable input (a budget) to produce two valuable outputs (target destruction potential and defense kill potential). The extension of this case to three or more outputs raises no new problems, although diagrammatic representation in two dimensions is no longer possible. If there are three outputs, the production-possibility and indifference curves become three-dimensional surfaces; if n, they are n-dimensional surfaces.

Problems involving two or more inputs do, however, require a somewhat different, although analogous, approach. Consider first the simplest of these, where there are two valuable inputs and only one valuable output. We might, as an example, take a subproblem of our first example, namely, the procurement of a strategic air force which will maximize target destruction. Suppose, for simplicity of analysis, that only two valuable inputs are required by a strategic air force—say bomber aircraft and bombs.[12] We will continue to assume, again grossly simplifying reality, that the output or objective of the strategic air force can be measured as a single dimension—expected number of targets destroyed. We may estimate by systematic quantitative analysis and plot the maximum potential destruction with varying numbers and combinations of bombs and bombers (see fig. 5). We estimate, say, that with 400

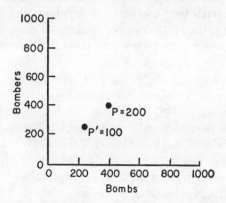

Figure 5.   Substitution between bombs and bombers.

---

[12] We will assume in this example that bombs must be paid for by the Air Force, as if the Atomic Energy Commission managed bomb production as an "industrial fund" or business. It is apparent that military forces should be planned *as if* bombs were costly inputs whether funds are actually transferred or not. See Stephen Enke, "Some Economic Aspects of Fissionable Material," *Quarterly Journal of Economics*, Vol. 68, May 1954, pp. 217–232.

bombs and 400 bombers the best we can achieve, with the best tactical employment of the bomber force, is the expected destruction of 200 targets, represented by point P (that is, we estimate that 50 per cent of the bombers, each armed with a bomb, will be attrited or will miss the target). Similarly, we estimate that it would take 250 bombs and 250 bombers to destroy 100 targets (point P') : the expected attrition rate will be higher with a smaller strike force.

With what other combinations of bombs and bombers can we expect to destroy 200 targets? Of course, with many possible combinations. As is typically the case in military (and other) operations, one valuable input may be substituted for another—within broad limits. There is no necessity to plan to use the same number of bombs and bombers. If the number of bombers exceeds the number of bombs, the aircraft not carrying bombs can serve a useful function as escorts, cutting down the attrition of the bomb carriers. If the number of bombs exceeds the number of bombers, some bombers can carry more than one bomb, attacking targets in sequence; or, alternatively, bombers surviving the first strike can be sent on a second. Of course, as we continue to substitute one input for the other, substitution will become more and more difficult. It will require at least 200 bombs to destroy 200 targets, no matter how many bombers we have at our disposal. Similarly some minimum number of aircraft will be needed to penetrate enemy defenses and deliver bombs on 200 targets, no matter how plentiful the bombs.

The locus of point P, showing the combinations of bombs and bombers which, with best tactical employment, can be expected to destroy 200 targets, is therefore a curve (known in economic theory as an "isoquant") convex to the origin and more or less asymptotic, at both extremes, to lines parallel to the X and Y axes (see fig. 6). The locus of the point P' (expected destruction = 100 targets) will be a curve of similar shape closer to the origin. Other isoquants can be estimated for any given level of expected target destruction—the best tactical employment being assumed for the combination of bombs and bombers represented by each point.

The use of resources is "efficient" in this case with a single valuable output or objective, where it is impossible to increase the output without increasing the use of at least one of the valuable inputs.

In figure 6 every point on each of the isoquants represents an efficient use of resources. It is therefore possible to move to a higher isoquant (that is, destroy more targets) only by increasing the use of at least one valuable input (bombs or bombers).

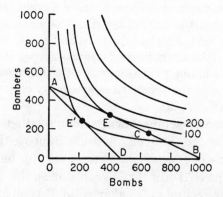

Figure 6.   Isoquants and exchange curves.

But which of this infinity of efficient points is *optimal?* In order to answer this question, we must have a measure of the relative costs [13] of bombs and bombers. Suppose, again for simplicity of exposition, that the costs of both bombs and bombers are constant, that two bombs can always be exchanged for one bomber. We can now immediately determine the optimal combination of bombs and bombers for any allocation of budget to the strategic air force. If the budget is sufficient to buy 500 bombers (all spent on bombers) or 1,000 bombs (all spent on bombs), the optimal combination of bombs and bombers to procure is represented by point E on figure 6. At this point the "exchange" curve (the straight line A-B) showing the combinations which may be procured with the given budget is tangent to a target isoquant—the highest isoquant which it can attain.

Let us go over the meaning of these curves again in order to make them clear. The exchange curve shows the way the inputs can be exchanged (in buying or producing them) while keeping the total budget constant. The isoquant shows the way the inputs can be substituted for each other while keeping the quantity of output constant. When the two curves are tangent, as at point E on figure 6, no further substitution of one input for the other can increase the output.[14] The only way to increase output in those circumstances would be to get a larger budget.

---

[13] The problems of defining the apropriate measure of costs are postponed to chapter VI.

[14] The slope of the exchange curve indicates the trade-offs possible in buying the inputs. It is the ratio of their marginal or incremental costs—the latter being the extra cost of buying an additional unit of each item. The slope of the isoquant similarly indicates the trade-offs possible in using the inputs. At the point of tangency these slopes, or trade-off possibilities, are equal.

Other points such as C on the exchange curve would be non-optimal. For exchange curves representing different budgets, there would be other optimal points, of course. The expected target destruction so calculated for all hypothetical budget allocations to the strategic air force (the budget being divided among inputs in each case in the optimal manner) was part of the information needed for the construction of the production-possibility curve in our first example, shown in figure 2.

A number of interesting and characteristic relations between inputs and outputs may be "read off" figure 6. Suppose that the price of bombs is higher—one bomb exchanging, say, for one bomber as in the exchange curve AD. In that circumstance, the optimal combination will tend to contain a smaller ratio of bombs to bombers, and appropriate tactics economizing on bombs will have to be used. With a higher price for bombs, the target destruction potential at any given budget level will be reduced, but not by as much if the ratio of bombs to bombers is optimally adjusted as if this ratio is left unchanged. We can also use this diagram to see how much the budget would have to be increased to maintain the same target destruction potential with a higher price for bombs: more bombers and fewer bombs would be purchased with the larger budget.

If the quantity of one input is limited (for example, if no more than, say, 300 bombs may be obtained from the Atomic Energy Commission at any price) the exchange curves become vertical at this point, as in figure 7. Increments of high budgets must all be spent on bombers, and tactics optimally adjusted to whatever bomb/bomber ratio results. Calculations of this kind can be used to estimate how much additional bomb production would be worth—in terms of bombers and therefore also in terms of dollars. In the hypothetical example shown in figure 7, the target destruction that can be achieved with a maximum of 300 bombs available and a budget equivalent to 600 bombers could be achieved with a budget equivalent to 500 bombers if bombs were continuously available at half the cost of bombers. In other words, the additional bombs would be "worth" 100 bombers more than their cost.

The extension of this case to three or more valuable inputs requires nothing more than the abandonment of plane geometry. Here let us turn to the use of economic analysis in the search for more efficient courses of action.

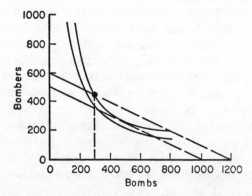

Figure 7.   Exchange curves with special constraints.

THE ELEMENTS OF AN ECONOMIC ANALYSIS

The essence of economic choice in military planning is not quantitative analysis: calculation may or may not be necessary or useful, depending upon the problem and what is known about it. The essential thing is the comparison of all the relevant alternatives from the point of view of the objectives each can accomplish and the costs which it involves; and the selection of the best (or a "good") alternative through the use of appropriate economic criteria.

The elements of a military problem of economic choice, whether its solution requires advanced mathematics, high speed computing equipment, or just straight hard thinking, are therefore the following:

1. An objective or objectives. What military (or other national) aim or aims are we trying to accomplish with the forces, equipments, projects, or tactics that the analysis is designed to compare? Choice of objectives is fundamental: if it is wrongly made, the whole analysis is addressed to the wrong question. For instance, we assumed in example 1 above that the sole objective of air defense is the slaughter of enemy aircraft: if in fact one of its major objectives is the early identification of an enemy attack and the provision of tactical warning to United States targets, the force we selected in example 1 is unlikely to be either optimal or efficient.

2. Alternatives. By what alternative forces, equipments, projects, tactics, and so on, may the objective be accomplished? The alternatives are frequently referred to as *systems* [15]

---

[15] Hence "systems analysis," a term frequently applied to complex quantitative analyses.

because each combines all the elements—men, machines, and the tactics of their employment—needed to accomplish the objective. System A may differ from System B in only one respect (for example, in number of bombs per bomber), or in several (number of bombs per bomber, number of strikes, and so on), but both are complete systems, however many elements they have in common. The great problem in choosing alternatives to compare is to be sure that all the good alternatives have been included. Frequently we lack the imagination to do this at the beginning of an analysis; we think of better alternatives (that is, invent new systems) as the analysis proceeds and we learn more about the problem. The invention of new and better systems in this fashion is indeed one of the principal payoffs from this kind of analysis.

3. Costs or resources used. Each alternative method of accomplishing the objective, or in other words each system, involves the incurring of certain costs or the using up of certain resources (these are different phrases to describe the same phenomena). Costs are the negative values in the analysis (as the objectives are positive values). The resources required may be general (as is commonly the case in problems of long-range planning), or highly specific (as in most tactical problems), or mixed. Some of the difficult problems of which costs to include and how to measure them are considered in chapter VI.

4. A model or models. Models are abstract representations of reality which help us to perceive significant relations in the real world, to manipulate them, and thereby predict others. They may take any of numerous forms. Some are small-scale physical representations of reality, like model aircraft in a wind tunnel. Many are simply representations on paper— like mathematical models. Or, finally, they may be simple sets of relationships that are sketched out in the mind and not formally put down on paper. In no case are models photographic reproductions of reality; if they were, they would be so complicated that they would be of no use to us. They have to abstract from a great deal of the real world—focusing upon what is relevant for the problem at hand, ignoring what is irrelevant. Whether or not one model is better than another depends not on its complexity, or its appearance of reality, but solely on whether it gives better predictions (and

thereby helps us to make better decisions).[16] In systems
analyses models of one type or another are required to trace
the relations between inputs and outputs, resources and objectives, for each of the systems to be compared, so that we
can predict the relevant consequences of choosing any system.

5. A criterion. By "criterion" we mean the test by which we
choose one alternative or system rather than another. The
choice of an appropriate economic criterion is frequently the
central problem in designing a systems analysis. In principle,
the criterion we want is clear enough: the optimal system
is the one which yields the greatest excess of positive values
(objectives) over negative values (resources used up, or
costs). But as we have already seen, this clear-cut ideal solution is seldom a practical possibility in military problems.[17]
Objectives and costs usually have no common measure: there
is no generally acceptable way to subtract dollars spent or
aircraft lost from enemy targets destroyed. Moreover, as in
two of the cases above, there may be multiple objectives or
multiple costs that are incommensurable. So in most military
analyses we have to be satisfied with some approximation
to the ideal criterion that will enable us to say, not that some
system A is optimal, but that it is better than some other proposed systems B, C, and so on. In many cases we will have
to be content with calculating efficient rather than optimal
systems, relying on the intuitive judgment of well-informed
people (of whom the analyst may be one) to select one of the
efficient systems in the neighborhood of the optimum. The
choice is the subject of chapter VI.

It cannot be stated too frequently or emphasized enough that economic choice is *a way of looking at problems* and does not necessarily depend upon the use of any analytic aids or computational
devices. Some analytic aids (mathematical models) and computing machinery are quite likely to be useful in analyzing complex
military problems, but there are many military problems in which
they have not proved particularly useful where, nevertheless, it is
rewarding to array the alternatives and think through their
implications in terms of objectives and costs. Where mathematical

---

[16] Bombardiers once bombed visually, using simple models in their heads to estimate the
bomb's trajectory in relation to the target. Modern bombsights use mathematical models, requiring high speed computers for solution, to make the same estimate. The model used by the
modern bombsight is better only if its predictions are more accurate—a question of fact
which has to be tested by experiment.

[17] In private industry this "ideal" criterion is the familiar one of profit maximization.

models and computations are useful, they are in no sense alternatives to or rivals of good intuitive judgment; they supplement and complement it: Judgment is always of critical importance in designing the analysis, choosing the alternatives to be compared, and selecting the criterion. Except where there is a completely satisfactory one-dimensional measurable objective (a rare circumstance), judgment must supplement the quantitative analysis before a choice can be recommended.

THE REQUIREMENTS APPROACH

In the absence of systematic analysis in terms of objectives and costs, a procedure that might be called the "requirements approach" is commonly used in the military departments and throughout much of the government. Staff officers inspect a problem, say, the defense of the continental United States or the design of the next generation of heavy bomber, draft a plan which seems to solve the problem, and determine requirements from the plan. Then feasibility is checked: Can the "required" performance characteristics, such as some designated speed and range, be achieved? Can the necessary budget be obtained? Does the nation have the necessary resources in total? If the program passes the feasibility tests, it is adopted; if it fails, some adjustments have to be made. But the question: What are the payoffs *and the costs* of alternative programs? may not be explicitly asked during the process of setting the requirement or deciding upon the budget. In fact, officials have on occasion boasted that their stated "requirements" have been based on need alone.

This, of course, is an illusion. Some notion of cost (money, resources, time), however imprecise, is implicit in the recognition of any limitation. Military departments frequently determine "requirements" which are from 10 to 25 per cent higher than the available budget, but never ten times as high, and seldom twice as high. But this notion of cost merely rules out grossly infeasible programs. It does not help in making optimal or efficient choices.

For that purpose it is essential that alternative ways of achieving military objectives be costed, and that choices be made on the basis of payoff and cost. How *are* choices made by military planners prior to any costing of alternatives? We have never heard any satisfying explanation. As we noted in our discussion of figure 6, a good or efficient choice depends upon the relative costs of different resources or inputs; there was no "good" bomb/bomber combination or tactic independent of cost. The derivation of requirements by any process that fails to cost alternatives can result in good solutions only by accident. Probably military planners sometimes weigh relative costs in some crude manner, at least subconsciously, even when they deny they do; or they make choices on the basis of considerations which ought to be secondary or tertiary, such as the preservation of an existing command structure, or the matching of a reported foreign accomplishment.

The defects of the requirements approach can be seen clearly if we think of applying it to our problems as a consumer. Suppose the consumer mulls over his transportation problem and decides, "on the basis of need alone," that he requires a new Cadillac. It is "the best" car he knows, and besides Jones drives one. So he buys a Cadillac, ignoring cost and ignoring therefore the sacrifices he is making in other directions by buying "the best." There are numerous alternative ways of solving the consumer's transportation problem (as there are always numerous ways of solving a military problem), and a little costing of alternatives prior to purchase might have revealed that the purchase of "the best" instrument is not *necessarily* an optimal choice. Perhaps if the consumer had purchased a Pontiac or a secondhand Cadillac he would have saved enough to maintain and operate it and take an occasional trip.[18] Or if he had purchased a Chevrolet he could have afforded to keep his old car and become head of a two-car family. One of these alternatives, properly costed and compared, might have promised a far greater amount of utility for the consumer than the purchase of a new Cadillac "on the basis of need alone." Or the exercise might have reassured the consumer that the new Cadillac was indeed optimal. While expensive unit equipment is not necessarily optimal, in some cases it can be proved to be.

THE PRIORITIES APPROACH

Another procedure that seems to have a great deal of appeal, in both military planning and other government activities, is the "priorities approach." To facilitate a decision about how to spend a specified budget, the desirable items are ranked according to the urgency with which they are needed. The result is a list of things that might be bought, the ones that are more important being near the top and the ones that are less important being near the bottom. Lists that rank several hundred weapons and items have sometimes been generated in the military services.

---

[18] Costing in our sense is never simply the cost of a unit of equipment; it is always the cost of a complete system including everything that must be purchased with the equipment and the cost of maintaining and operating it. See the next section below.

At first blush, this appears to be a commendable and systematic way to tackle the problem. When one reflects a bit, however, the usefulness and significance of such a list begins to evaporate. Consider the following items ranked according to their (hypothetical) priorities: (1) Missile X, (2) Radar device Y, (3) Cargo aircraft Z. How do you use such a ranking? Does it mean that the entire budget should be spent on the first item? Probably not, for it is usually foolish to allocate all of a budget to a single weapon or object. Besides, if a budget is to be so allocated, the ranking of the items below the first one has no significance.

Does the ranking mean that the money should go to the first item until no additional amount is needed, then to the second item until no further amount is needed, and so on? Hardly, because there could be some need for more of Missile X almost without limit. Even if only a limited amount of Missile X was available, to keep buying right out to this limit would usually be a foolish rule. After quite a few Missile X's were purchased, the next dollar could better be spent on some other item. Even using lifeboats for women and children first is foolish if a sailor or doctor on each lifeboat can save many lives.

Perhaps a priority list means that we should spend more money on the higher-priority items than on those having a lower priority. But this makes little sense, since some of the items high on the list, for example, the radar device, may cost little per unit and call at most for a relatively small amount of money; while some lower-ranking purchases, such as the cargo aircraft, may call for comparatively large sums if they are to be purchased at all. In any event, the priorities reveal nothing about how much more should be spent on particular items.

Just how anyone can use such a list is not clear. Suppose a consumer lists possible items for his monthly budget in the order of their priority and he feels that in some sense they rank as follows: (1) groceries, (2) gas and oil, (3) cigarettes, (4) repairs to house, (5) liquor, and (6) steam baths. This does not mean that he will spend all of his funds on groceries, nor does it mean that he will spend nothing on liquor or steam baths. His problem is really to allocate his budget among these different objects. He would like to choose the allocation such that an extra dollar on cigarettes is just as important to him as an extra dollar on groceries. At the margin, therefore, the objects of expenditure would be equally important (except for those that are not purchased at all).

The notion of priority stems from the very sensible proposition that one should do "first things first." It makes sense, or at least the top priority does, when one considers the use of a small increment of resources or time. If one thinks about the use of an extra dollar or of the next half-hour of his time, it is sensible to ask, "What is the most urgent—the first-priority—item?" If one is deciding what to do with a budget or with the next eight hours, however, he ordinarily faces a problem of *allocation*, not of setting priorities. A list of priorities does not face the problem or help solve it.

Thus in formulating defense policy and choosing weapon systems, we have to decide how much effort or how many resources should go to each item. The "priorities approach" does not solve the allocation problem and can even trap us into adopting foolish policies.[19]

SOME MISUNDERSTANDINGS

There is some resistance to the use of economic analysis in military problems that is based on misunderstanding.

An economically efficient solution to military problems does not imply a cheap force or a small military budget. It simply implies that whatever the military budget (or other limitation, for example, on personnel) the greatest military capabilities are developed. Since military capabilities are plural and not easily commensurate, an efficient military establishment, in the technical sense, would merely be one in which no single capability—antisubmarine, ground warfare, offensive air, and so on—could be increased without decreasing another. An optimal establishment would in addition have the right "balance" among capabilities —a harder problem for analysis.

From the point of view of the nation, of the military establishment as a whole,[20] and of the Treasury Department, the achievement of efficiency and the approach to an optimal solution can be a common objective. There is a conflict of interest between the Treasury, the Bureau of the Budget, and economy-minded Congressmen on the one hand, and the military services on the other when the level of the budget is in question. The military services always (and properly) want more; the economizers always (and also properly) offer resistance, or try to impose reductions. But

---

[19] For a revealing discussion of priority lists, see *Military Construction Appropriations for 1958*, Hearings before the Subcommittee of the Committee on Appropriations, House of Representatives, 85th Congress, 1st Session, U.S. Government Printing Office, Washington, D.C., 1957, 420–427.

[20] There are undoubtedly sectional interests within the military—particularly commands, services, and staff units—which might suffer from increased efficiency in the establishment as a whole, and have therefore a perverse incentive to prevent efficiency.

once the budget has been determined, there is no longer conflict of interest.

In fact the choices that maximize military capability for a given budget are the same choices that minimize the cost of attaining that capability. As we shall see in chapter VI, the capability-maximizing criterion (given budget) and cost-minimizing criterion (given capability) are logically equivalent and therefore lead to the same choices and the same programs (for any given scale of operations, as determined by either budget or capability). If an Atlas missile system maximizes our strategic air power for a given SAC budget, it also minimizes the cost of providing that much strategic air power.

Some officers object to economic analysis because they think it implies cheap equipment, or the continued use of obsolescent equipment. This is by no means the case except, properly, where the use of cheap or old equipment results in lower system cost. New equipment does tend, on a unit basis, to be more expensive than old; but this does not mean that its use is uneconomic, any more than the use of modern more expensive equipment is necessarily uneconomic in industry. What counts, in the military as in industry, is not the unit cost of procurement, but the total system cost—the cost of procuring and maintaining and operating the whole system in which the new equipment is embedded—of achieving an appropriate capability or objective. This may be greater or less with new, more "expensive," higher performance equipment. In the case of the atomic bomb it was much less, although the bombs themselves are presumably much more expensive. There is no presumption that the substitution of the "expensive" B–47 for the "cheap" B–29 was uneconomic. The problem of the relative worths and costs of quality and quantity is, in the military as in private industry, an economic problem, amenable to economic calculus.

Another misunderstanding is reflected in the question, "What do dollars matter when national survival is at stake?" They matter precisely because they represent (however imperfectly in some circumstances) generalized national resources at the disposal of the military. Unless they are economically used, resources will be wasted, and the nation will have less military capability and a smaller chance of survival. If any one dimension of military power is wastefully planned, that is, at greater than minimum cost, some other dimension will, with a given total military budget, have fewer resources at its disposal and necessarily less capability.

Of course waste can be compensated, within limits, by voting higher military budgets at the expense of non-military objectives, but legislatures are understandably less than willing to raise budgets for this purpose. If they vote a higher budget, they want the still greater military capability that an economic use of the higher budget would make possible.

EFFICIENCY IN THE LARGE VERSUS EFFICIENCY IN THE SMALL

It is convenient in analyzing national security problems (and many others) to distinguish between "efficiency in the large" and "efficiency in the small." (Efficiency in this section will again be used in the general sense of "making good use" of resources—not in the technical sense defined earlier in the chapter.) Efficiency in the large, or at relatively high levels, involves getting the gross allocations right in reference to major objectives—in the case of national security, the allocation of resources between military and non-military uses, and allocations to the Services and the major military "missions" in conformity with national objectives. Efficiency in the small, or at relatively low levels, involves making good use of the resources allocated to each mission and the numerous subordinate jobs within each.

Quantitative economic analysis can be useful in both types of problems, although the type of analysis that is appropriate in the two cases is likely to differ. Typically in decisions at relatively high levels there are important qualitative or intangible factors which make it impossible to define a satisfactory criterion and therefore impossible to devise an explicit model which points the way to *the* right decision.[21] Nevertheless the explicit use of models and of quantitative analysis is not only possible in many such problems, but essential if good solutions are to be found.

Take as an example the division of the budget for the strategic air war between offense and defense. This is a comparatively high level problem, beset by intangibles. On one side is the mystique of the offense—the conviction of military services everywhere that morale depends upon offense-mindedness, and that reliance on defensive measures is self-defeating. On the other side is the morale and resolve of the civilian nation: will it dare to threaten war if it is defenseless against enemy bombs? And in between is that most pervasive of all intangibles—the mind of the enemy. How does it function, and what will deter him?

---

[21] Some lower level problems are in this respect precisely like the high level ones.

Nevertheless, quantitative calculations are essential to a rational solution. Calculations can show that with the expenditure of a tolerable number of billions of dollars annually on an offensive force *and on the defense of the offensive force,* we can with high confidence (say, 90 per cent) guarantee effective retaliation against an aggressor and therefore that a rational aggressor will be deterred. Similar calculations can show how this total deterrent budget should be divided between the offensive force and various protective devices including warning nets, hardening of installations, and interceptor and missile defenses.

At the same time, calculations can show that much larger budgets (beyond the range of practical politics) will provide only partial and uncertain (low-confidence) protection in the event deterrence fails.

Calculations of this kind, whether made explicitly or implicitly, account for the prevalent view, undoubtedly correct in present circumstances (1960), that protected offensive deterrent power has first claim on the national security budget. For what we are trying to do in allocating between offense and defense is to minimize some combination of (a) the chance that all-out thermonuclear war will occur, and (b) the amount of damage we will suffer if it does occur.[22] While we do not know precisely what combination we want to minimize, we can as a first approximation regard it as the product of (a) and (b). We would be willing to reallocate budget from deterrent forces to protective ones like Nikes or civilian shelters only if the expected damage to us if war occurs was reduced by a greater factor than the chance of war was increased.

Of course, we cannot make a complete, explicit calculation of such a product, for we do not have a direct measure of the chance of war. The final stage in allocating funds between deterrent and survival measures is a task for judgment, but judgment's task can be greatly facilitated by calculations showing how accomplishments of the proximate objectives, that is, ability to inflict damage and ability to survive attack, are related to budget expenditures.

If the technical possibilities of offense and defense, as reflected in the budget costs of buying given amounts of deterrent power and protection, were drastically altered by, say, some technological breakthrough in defense, our judgment about the best allocation would also change. Suppose that, both for the Russians and ourselves, the relations were more or less reversed, so that at practical budget levels we could buy a high-confidence, virtually leak-

---

[22] The amount of damage we will be able to inflict on the enemy is implicit in the calculation, since that *is* our means of deterring war.

proof defense; while the similar effectiveness of the Russian defense made the task of providing an effective retaliatory force tremendously uncertain and expensive. We are sure that in these circumstances men of good judgment would assign top priority to providing the curtain of death rays that would kill incoming bombers, missiles, and bombs. On the other hand our strategic bombing forces, in fighting for appropriations for their low-confidence mission, would find themselves in the same difficult, uncomfortable position that Continental Air Defense and the agencies responsible for civil defense now occupy.

Of course *priority* provides no clue to the proportion of the budget to be allocated to the deterrence mission—except when the total budget is small. When the budget is large, the best proportions depend upon the effects of *increments* of budget spent on deterrence and survival respectively (and these effects are calculable).

As we descend to lower levels of decision making, there is frequently a change in the proportion of quantitative and qualitative factors that affords greater scope for explicit analysis. If the problem is not how much to allocate to air defense relative to other missions, but with which of two proposed electronic gun sights to equip fighter aircraft, the relevance and necessity of quantitative analysis becomes obvious. To make a rational choice we must, at the least, have quantitative evidence on accuracy, reliability, cost and availability, weight and the consequences of added weight, and so on. Of course the great majority of problems of military choice are, like this one, lower level problems, which are decided in the first instance at levels in the departmental or military hierarchy well below the top.

The bulk of explicit quantitative analysis so far attempted in the military, chiefly by operations analysis groups, has been directed toward such lower level problems, and this will probably always be true, and it may be desirable. Not only do the lower level problems demand quantitative analysis and appear more "manageable"; they are, in the aggregate, of great importance. Experienced operations researchers report that they frequently discover that some of the systems which they compare are better by large factors—three, four or more—than others seriously proposed, sometimes with enthusiastic advocates. This should come as no surprise to economists who have studied international differences in productivity and costs, or even differences among enterprises within a nation. There are many ways to make any product or achieve any objective, and some are much more efficient than others. In the absence of an adequate economic calculus, highly inefficient ways can be and are chosen.[23]

The usual task of quantitative analysis is the improvement of decisions at relatively low levels in the military hierarchy—efficiency in the small. But while decisions at these levels appear more susceptible to quantitative analysis, and indeed frequently are, such analysis presents peculiar and formidable difficulties. These are associated with the choice of criteria, and will be more fully discussed in chapter VI. What follows here is an impressionistic introduction to the nature of the problem.

In the first place, for a lower level analysis to be more manageable, it must be confined to a lower level context. Many of the things that would be treated as variables in a higher level analysis —specifically, decisions at still higher levels and at the same levels in other branches of the military—must be taken as given. The systems to be compared in the analysis, while "complete" in some sense, must be limited, with only a few elements varying from system to system.

Analyses so confined to lower level contexts, which assume decisions given at higher and collateral levels, are called "sub-optimizations." [24] They attempt to find optimal (or near optimal) solutions, but to subproblems rather than to the whole problem of the organization in whose welfare or utility we are interested. If a consumer tries to solve his transportation problem (Cadillac vs. Chevrolet) more or less in isolation, taking other major decisions affecting his income and expenditure as given, he is sub-optimizing. If the Air Force tries to decide between two gun sights for fighters, taking the general organization, size and tactics of fighter defense as given, it is sub-optimizing. If we are taking a Departmental or Service point of view, we sub-optimize when we try to solve a problem at a level lower than that of the Secretary or Chief of Staff. From a national point of view, even problems at the Chief of Staff level, in a context coextensive with the responsibilities of the Service, must be regarded as sub-optimizations.

Sub-optimizations are both necessary and inevitable, and provide scope for productive quantitative analyses of important problems of choice. But they are hard to do well. While analysis appears

---

[23] We are not suggesting, of course, that *all* international or intercompany differences in productivity measure differences in the efficiency of utilization of resources. Where labor is a relatively cheap factor it will usually be efficient to choose methods which result in lower average labor productivity. But the differences do measure the wide range of alternative methods and therefore the range of possible error if economic rationale is lacking.

[24] Sub-optimizations correspond to the partial equilibrium analyses of conventional economic theory.

to become more manageable as we move to lower levels, limit the context, and restrict the scope within which systems vary, three inter-related problems tend to become more formidable the further we move in this direction:

1. The first is the problem of selecting an appropriate criterion —appropriate, that is, to the level at which the decision is being studied—that is consistent with higher level criteria, and ultimately with the welfare of the organization or group in which we are really interested. It is very easy to choose some proximate criterion in a low level problem that is inconsistent with higher level criteria—to take a previous example, maximizing air defense kill potential when an equally important or more important function of air defense is to provide adequate warning.

2. The second we will call the problem of spillovers; and this too we will discuss at greater length in Chapter VI. When we confine analysis within narrow contextual limits, there is always a possibility that some of the consequences may affect—favorably or unfavorably—other parts of the larger organization or group with whose welfare we are concerned. Certain SAC deployments will facilitate, and others will make more difficult, the task of the air defense system in providing warning to and defense of SAC bases. These spillover effects would be missed in an analysis narrowly confined to SAC.

3. Third, there is the problem of choosing the context and the elements that will be permitted to vary in the systems compared. The context need not, and indeed normally should not, be as restricted as the area of immediate decision that provides the *focus* of the analysis. The broader the context the less the danger from inconsistent criteria and the less likely it is that significant spillover effects will be missed. The broader the context, too, the fewer other decisions one needs to take as given, and the greater opportunity one has to explore the interdependence of decisions at different and collateral levels. But breadth of context and any increase in the number of variables have to be purchased by drastically increasing the complexity of the analysis,[25] with all this im-

---

[25] The number of cases to be computed and compared increases as the power of the number of interdependent variables. If we let each variable take four alternative values and have two variables, the number of cases is 4^2 or 16—a back-of-the-envelope problem. If we increase the number of variables to 10, we have to compute 4^{10} cases, or more than a million, and probably need a high speed electronic computer.

plies in terms of research manpower, expense, and time. So we don't want to expand context or increase variables unnecessarily.

How large should the context be? How many decisions should be analyzed simultaneously? There are no rules except—be aware of the dangers, and use good sense to reduce them. Some low level problems are "factorable," that is, good decisions don't depend much upon other decisions, and spillovers aren't too important. Where problems are relatively factorable, the context can be kept small and the variables few. One can frequently minimize the cost of one operation without much affecting others. But other problems simply aren't factorable in this sense. Their solution, even if responsibility is fixed at a low level in the hierarchy, has wide ramifications. And any optimal solution must take account of the interdependence of this problem and others. As an obvious and extreme example, an analysis of the location of SAC bases cannot be successfully sub-optimized even at the level of SAC Headquarters. Their location not only has spillovers on air defense, as we have seen, and on our ability to fight local wars in various parts of the world; but it may also affect the whole structure of our alliances. We must either optimize on a fairly grand scale (probably impossible in any explicit quantitative manner), or frankly label our sub-optimization a partial analysis, dealing only with *some* of the factors important to a decision.

Consider another hypothetical example, mentioned above, which demands, in the design of the analysis, some compromises between desirable breadth of context and the need to keep research requirements within practical limits. Suppose the analyst's assignment is to select the "best" of several proposed electronic gun sights for fighter aircraft. How large a context should he assume in the study? How many other decisions should he assume to be given?

At one extreme he might fit the sights into very small systems— say specific fighter aircraft—and "score" them by the number of hits registered in tests on tow targets. Would this give him the right answer? Not necessarily. In the first place the criterion may not be closely related to the real task of fighter aircraft. The sights (or some of them) may be heavy enough to affect the plane's range, or its speed or maneuverability. The number of tubes in the electronic system would affect the reliability and the ease of maintenance of the weapons system. Furthermore, performance in combat situations might not be taken sufficiently into account in comparing the number of hits on a tow target.

To overcome some of these shortcomings, the analyst might enlarge the context slightly and fit each gun sight into a fighter plane in combat (on paper) with an enemy aircraft. Would it be in accordance with higher level aims to put this particular emphasis on victory in individual duels? Again, not necessarily. The best gun sight in a duel of one against one would probably turn out to be an extremely expensive one, making it necessary, with a given budget, to sacrifice numbers (or perhaps the range of the fighter). The electronic gear might cause too many aborts (planes that return to base unable to complete their mission) or keep too many planes on the ground. From the standpoint of numerical superiority, number of interceptions, and other aspects of the whole fighter operation, this gun sight might be a poor choice indeed.

The analyst appears to be driven to larger and larger systems—fitting the gun sights into planes, then the planes into fighter groups, then the groups into relevant military operations. He may even want to ask what tasks or budgets make sense in view of the whole military operation and of political realities. But while larger systems analyses make his criterion problem (or one aspect of it) more manageable, they become more cumbersome and more aggregative. At some point in the process, depending on many circumstances (how much time he has, what research resources he has, what chance he or his organization has of influencing higher or collateral decisions, how important the choice among gun sights is anyway?), he must accept a limited context and a less-than-perfect proximate criterion, try to keep aware, in a general and qualitative way, of its shortcomings and biases, treat effects outside his system crudely, and get on with his inevitable job of sub-optimizing.

KINDS OF MILITARY DECISIONS

Military decisions may be classified by kind as well as by level. For purposes of economic analysis it is frequently useful to distinguish:

Operations decisions (strategy and tactics)
Procurement or force composition decisions
Research and development decisions.

The basic difference among these kinds of decisions, from the point of view of analysis, is the time at which the decision affects the capability of the military forces concerned. An operations decision (how many destroyers to use per convoy) can affect operations and capability almost immediately; in fact, analyses and decisions focused on operations are usually concerned with the near future. A decision to procure something, on the other hand, cannot affect capability until the thing procured has been produced (in the case of manpower, trained) and fitted into operational forces. If the thing is an aircraft carrier or a bomber, the time involved may be many years. Decisions to develop something tend to affect capabilities at an even later date—after the thing has been developed, and produced, and then fitted into operational forces.

An economic analysis, whether quantitative or qualitative, will usually attempt to determine the utility of alternative systems by examining the effect on military capabilities, whenever these occur. The effects of a change in tactics in 1960 can perhaps be fully evaluated in the context of 1960. But to evaluate the effects of a decision in 1960 to develop (or even to procure) a new missile may require projecting the context to 1970 or later. Analyses based on long-range forecasts are, of course, highly uncertain, and this fact drastically alters the form of analysis which it is sensible and useful to make and the kind of conclusions one can draw from it.

In an operations decision, the relevant resource constraints are usually specific rather than general, simply because the time horizon is so short. If the problem involves the tactics of convoying, the escort vessels that have to be used must probably be taken as given—in number, speed, armament, and so on. No budget however large can produce more in the short run. Similarly, SAC's emergency war plans for a retaliatory strike must utilize specific planes carrying specific bombs from specific bases. The fact that the appropriate resource constraints are specific by no means inhibits economic analysis. We have seen that the problem of making economic use of a number of specific resources is fundamentally the same problem as making economic use of a single general resource, although the calculations may be more complicated. In fact, the first large-scale explicit use of quantitative economic analysis in military problems by operations research groups in the Second World War was directed toward problems of tactical operations. Serious attempts to apply the same techniques to longer-range procurement and development problems, in which constraints are more appropriately one or a very few general resources, followed much later.

Analysis focused on a *procurement* decision (for example, which of two missiles to order in 1960) almost of necessity will have to study *operations* in later years—the strategy and tactics with which each missile will be used after it has been introduced into the force. For a valid comparison, each must be used in the most effective way in the context of the appropriate future year. (Similarly, an analysis focused on a development decision may, in order to gauge potential payoffs, study procurement and operations as well.) The analysis of a procurement problem is, however, solely directed toward the procurement decision in the immediate future; its analysis of future tactics is incidental to choice of bomber; it is tentative and leads to no recommendations about tactics. The time to make analyses focused on tactical decisions in 1968 is not earlier than 1967.

VI

THE CRITERION PROBLEM

In the earlier chapter we stated that the selection of an appropriate criterion is frequently the central problem in the design of an economic analysis intended to improve military decisions. Whatever the particular problem, military or civilian, it is fairly obvious that, in choosing among alternative means to our ends, we need to scan the ends themselves with a critical eye. New techniques or types of equipment may be extremely efficient in achieving certain aims, but these aims may be the wrong ones—aims that are selected almost unconsciously or at least without sufficient critical thought.

But to say that we should scrutinize our ultimate ends carefully in deciding upon the best course of action is much too vague. Suppose we wish to choose among various motorcars. Merely to name and list the things we ultimately value (such as growth, approval, security, freedom, leisure, goods) is not very helpful in solving the problem. It is wise to think about such a list, for it may prevent us from making some absurd choice that does not contribute to *any* of these things, but in most situations the list provides little counsel. One reason it fails to do so is the tremendous gap between gas consumption, wheel base, and new seat covers, on the one hand, and leisure, security, and approval, on the other. This gap has to be at least partially bridged in order to reach any conclusions about policies. Another reason is the necessity of trading part of one desideratum for some of another, sacrificing faster "pick-up" for improved fuel consumption or giving up some comforts for a little more leisure.

Similarly, the mere enumeration of objectives in choosing among weapon systems, while it may be pertinent, does not serve as a guide to specific action. The objectives may include target destruction potential, invulnerability to enemy attack, strengthening of alliances, and reliability—all to be achieved "as soon as possible." All of these things would indeed be nice to have. But while good intentions are sometimes reputed to be excellent paving materials, in themselves they do not pave the way to preferred action. In practical problems of military (or other) choice there are always constraints which prevent us from simultaneously achieving all our objectives.

CRITERIA

Hence, in choosing among alternatives, we do more than to list things which it would be nice to have. Explicitly or implicitly we adopt criteria or tests of preferredness. One essential step in the analysis is predicting the consequences of alternative actions or systems—a step which, as indicated earlier, involves the use of sets of relationships called models. Another vital step is distinguishing preferred combinations of consequences from less desirable ones; this step entails the use of criteria. Thus, after having the features of different cars spelled out, the chooser has to decide what is the best combination of features. He may want the car that has maximum acceleration while meeting specific constraints on other aspects of performance and on cost. If so, that is his criterion. Or he may compare the features (including cost implications) of different cars subjectively and reach his decision. If so, the criterion is never made explicit, but is presumably the maximization of some function constrained by the chooser's limited resources.

There are times when the terms "criterion" appears to be a misnomer. For, on occasion, as we have seen, analysis can unravel only *some* of the consequences of alternative actions and exhibit these consequences to decision-makers after the usual manner of consumers' research.[1] (By this term we mean the kind of research that is often done to help consumers choose an item such as an automobile or a refrigerator.) Insofar as this is the case, a partial criterion (comparison in terms of selected consequences) may be used. There is then no problem of devising a definitive test, but there is the closely related problem of deciding *what* consequences the decision-maker should know about. In other situations, however, the analyst may be able (or may try) to trace out all the significant effects and learn enough about the decision-maker's preferences to evaluate those effects. In these instances, quantitative analysis *per se* may be used to pick out and recommend preferred courses of action. Insofar as this is the case, a definitive test of preferredness is necessary, and the criterion problem is the devising of that test. Most of the discussion that follows will relate

---

[1] Consumers' research publications sometimes recommend a single "best buy," using a criterion which may or may not be acceptable to a particular subscriber. But usually they content themselves with describing features and analyzing certain consequences, letting the subscriber supply (a total or final) evaluation and make the choice.

directly to the criterion problem faced in the latter situations, but much of it will pertain, at least indirectly, to the selection of partial criteria, that is, of selected effects that are relevant to the comparison of alternative actions.

The Necessity for Using "Proximate" Criteria

Ideally we should choose that course of action which, with available resources, maximizes something like the "satisfaction" of an individual, the profits of a firm, the "military worth" of the military establishment, or the "well-being" of a group. If possible, we should like to ascertain the total amount of these magnitudes under each of various alternative policies. Then we would pick the policy that promised to yield the most satisfaction, the most profits, the most military worth, or the most well-being, depending on the identity of the person or organization whose choice we were advising. But this prescription usually helps little more than saying that we want the best. Nobody knows precisely how satisfaction and military worth are related to the observable outcomes of various courses of action. We do not have the ability to translate outcomes into such terms. In practical problem-solving, therefore, we have to look at some "proximate" criterion which serves to reflect what is happening to satisfaction or military worth. Actual criteria are the practicable substitutes for the maximization of whatever we would ultimately like to maximize.

In comparisons of military operations or equipment, what is desired is the course of action that would contribute most to "winning" or deterring some kind (or kinds) of war, or even more generally, to achieving national security. Since it will usually be impossible to measure achievements in any of these terms, it is necessary to adopt indirect but workable criteria that appear to be consistent with ultimate aims.

Sub-Optimization and Criteria

The need to use proximate rather than ultimate tests opens the door to the selection of incorrect criteria. But the door is really swung wide open—in fact one might say that the welcome mat is put out—by another fact of life stressed in chapter V: the fact that problems of choice must be broken down into component pieces or sub-problems.

Let us examine this difficulty in somewhat greater detail. A military service (or government department or large corporation) cannot possibly have one man or one committee examine *all* its problems of choice simultaneously and pick each course of action in the light of all other decisions. It is inevitable that decision-making be broken into pieces. The division is almost necessarily along hierarchical lines, some of the broader policy choices being made by high level officials or groups, others being delegated to lower levels.[2]

Similarly, analyses must be piecemeal, since it is impossible for a single analysis to cover all problems of choice simultaneously in a large organization. Thus comparisons of alternative courses of action always pertain to a part of the government's (or corporation's) problem. Other parts of the over-all problem are temporarily put aside, possible decisions about some matters being ignored, specific decisions about others being taken for granted. The resulting analyses are intended to provide assistance in finding optimal, or at least good, solutions to sub-problems: in the jargon of systems analysis and operations research, they are suboptimizations.

Note again, however, that the scope of analysis does not have to, and indeed usually should not, coincide with the scope of authority in decision-making. Take the case of military decisions within the government. Analysis of a problem in antisubmarine warfare may have to be made in the context of a global war involving all services and the national economy, even though it is relevant to decisions within one bureau of the Navy Department. Fortunately no single authority runs the whole executive-legislative-judicial process in the United States government, but this does not mean that individual departments and subordinate units should not, on occasion, take a broad national point of view ("context" and criterion) in making decisions for which it is responsible in the hierarchy. The situation in a private corporation is precisely analogous. The individual division or department of the corporation, in making certain decisions delegated to it, will be expected to take a corporationwide point of view, tracing the full consequences of its actions on all operations of the firm.[3] The sales department is not

---

[2] We must again stress that no connotation of greater or lesser significance should be associated with these terms "higher" and "lower" levels. The lower level decisions may in some circumstances be the more important ones. Choosing the best bomber-missile systems and the means of protecting them, for example, may do more to enhance our deterrent force than allocating more funds to the Air Force to buy inferior systems.

[3] The exceptions in which individual divisions (e.g., those of General Motors and U.S. Steel) are instructed to act autonomously and ignore the possible repercussions of their actions on the profits of other divisions of the corporation, are instructive. In these cases the corporation has deliberately decided that the "spillover" effects on other divisions are less important in the long run than the advantages of fixing responsibility and providing strong, clear-cut incentives. There is probably also a fear that the use of corporation-wide criteria in analysis may inevitably lead to an undesirable centralization of decision-making itself—a sort of "spillover" effect of a different kind. In any event, these exceptions are usually limited to certain kinds of decisions. Divisions of General Motors are supposed to be completely autonomous in buying and selling, but not in financing and therefore not in decisions requiring major capital expenditures. There are useful analogies in all this for the military.

expected to choose actions which maximize sales, or sales minus selling costs, but the total profits of the corporation—sales and other receipts minus all costs in all departments.

Piecemeal analysis and decision making have great advantages, some of which have already been stated. Small problems tend to be more "manageable" in a number of senses. As problems are broken down into smaller chunks, more detail can be taken into account by both researchers and decision-makers. In large firms a degree of decentralization greater than that which is inevitable is usually believed to be desirable so that the "man on the spot" can decide about many matters—and be held responsible for them.[4] In analysis, somewhat similarly, considerable breakdown of the problems of a corporation or a government department may be desirable so that the models used in estimating outcomes can be "on the spot," that is, less aggregative and more precise in their predictions than global or firm-wide models would be.

Finally, better hedging against uncertainty *may* result from breaking big problems into smaller ones. The difficulties that stem from inherent uncertainties will be discussed mostly in the next chapter, but a few words are in order here. If decision making is decentralized to a considerable extent, it may help against the possibility of getting stuck with lopsided views at the top. In civil government it has long been widely recognized that some separation of powers and dispersal of authority are important, partly as a hedging device. And in analysis, a degree of suboptimization *may* mean, for some problems, less risk of tying all analytical results to a "bad" criterion, for instance, one involving a spuriously specific objective in which uncertainty is neglected.

On the other hand, there is a real danger in piecemeal analysis, one whose importance must be reemphasized because it is probably not as widely appreciated as are the difficulties inherent in biting off too big a chunk of the problem. The danger is that the criteria adopted in lower level problems may be unrelated to and inconsistent with higher level criteria. As mentioned before, proximate criteria have to be used in any case; but since problems must be considered one piece at a time, a whole hierarchy of proximate criteria comes into play, and potential inconsistencies are abundant.

---

[4] This not only takes advantage of the man-on-the-spot's familiarity with the details of a problem but also constitutes a more desirable decision-making process anyway, getting more persons in the habit of using ingenuity and taking responsibility. Indeed this is of major importance for the functioning of the economy, and probably of equal importance in the military services.

An an example from the military sphere, suppose that the military establishes a requirement for 90 per cent reliability in the functioning of its weapon systems. Bows and arrows may pass such a test with flying colors, yet hand grenades may accomplish much more at the same cost, even if half of them are duds. Perhaps 90 per cent or 50 or 99 per cent has some intuitive appeal, but this gives little assurance that it is a sensible "requirement," criterion, or test. The point is that even plausible criteria for choosing lower level policies may not harmonize with higher level tests, that is, may not be in agreement with what we really want to do. Earlier we criticized the widespread practice in government of setting "requirements" without looking explicitly at costs. Because problems must be taken up piecemeal, there is danger that requirements will be set without looking .critically at payoffs either. And the achievement of a blindly selected "requirement" (even at minimum cost)[5] is likely to be inconsistent with higher level aims.

In a free enterprise economy we have a price mechanism and a system of incentives which, imperfectly but pervasively, enforce some measure of consistency between the lower level criteria used by individuals and firms in making their economic decisions and certain higher level criteria appropriate to the economy. A whole branch of economic theory, rather unfortunately labeled "welfare economics," is concerned with relations between high and low level economic criteria.[6] Under certain circumstances (the most important being absence of monopoly, free movement of factors of production, "full employment," and no external economies or diseconomies), the maximization of their own preference functions by individuals and of their own profits by firms will lead to an "efficient" use of resources in the economy—in the precisely defined senses that it will be impossible to produce more of any one good or service without producing less of some other *and* that it will be impossible to improve the satisfaction of any one individual

---

[5] Admittedly, if the requirement *has* to be taken as given, it is better to achieve it at minimum cost than at higher cost. Even a "bad" sub-optimization may be better than none at all. It may not make sense in the total context to raise the reliability of hand grenades to a magic 90%, but if it has to be so raised, the fewer resources we use in doing so the more will be available for sensible products.

[6] The classic work in this field is A. C. Pigou, *The Economics of Welfare*, 1st ed., Macmillan and Co., London, 1920. For an introductory and somewhat more modern exposition, see J. E. Meade and C. J. Hitch, *Introduction to Economic Analysis and Policy*, Oxford University Press, New York, 1938, especially Part II. For developments in, and qualifications to, the theory of welfare economics, see Paul A. Samuelson, *Foundations of Economic Analysis*, Harvard University Press, Cambridge, Mass., 1948, pp. 203–253; Kenneth J. Arrow, *Social Choice and Individual Values*, John Wiley and Son, New York, 1951; and R. C. Lipsey and K. Lancaster, "The General Theory of Second Best," *Review of Economic Studies*, 1956–57, pp. 11–32.

without reducing that of another.[7] Since, in general, firms do try to maximize profits and individuals do try to maximize preference functions, there will be a tendency for resources to be efficiently used in the economy to the extent that the assumed circumstances are approximated.

This is an interesting and, within limits, a useful conclusion. It might be regarded as equally plausible, or even more plausible, that the higher level economic criterion would require firms to minimize cost per unit of output (the ratio of cost to output) or to maximize productivity per head or per man-hour (the ratio of output to some one input) instead of maximizing profits (receipts minus costs). In fact both these criteria have been widely used—in some cases appropriately, in others not—as indexes of efficiency in comparisons between firms and countries. But it can be demonstrated that maximizing either of the ratios by firms in choosing methods of production, scale of operations, and so on, would result in an inefficient use of resources in the economy.

SOME CRITERION ERRORS

In the military (and indeed in the government generally) there is no comparable mechanism that tends to insure consistency between high level and low level criteria.[8] Since piecemeal analysis (sub-optimization) and therefore the use of low level criteria cannot be avoided, the prevention of even gross errors in the selection of criteria requires hard thought. In a very general sense all criterion errors involve inconsistency between the tests that are selected in analyzing lower level problems and the tests that are applicable at higher levels. However, some of the mistakes that occur most frequently have special characteristics and can be put into categories.

Maximizing Gain While Minimizing Cost

The consequences of an action fall into two types—(1) those positive gains which we like to increase, or the achievement of objectives, and (2) those negative effects which we like to decrease, or the incurrence of costs. Neither type by itself can serve as an adequate criterion: the maximizing of gains without regard to cost or resource limitation is hardly a helpful test, and the

---

[7] Of course efficiency in this sense does not imply an "optimal" distribution of income from anyone's point of view or an "optimal" rate of growth. Efficiency is not a sufficient condition for an optimum, but it does enable us to identify improvements in many situations.

[8] There are administrative devices—committees, special staffs at higher levels, etc.—which attempt, through cooperation and "coordination," to mitigate the consequences of the absence of such a mechanism.

minimizing of cost regardless of other consequences of the alternative actions is nonsense. Hence both gains and costs must appear in criteria but, as will be seen, they can make their appearance in various ways.

One ubiquitous source of confusion is the attempt to maximize gain while minimizing cost or, as a variant, the attempt to maximize two types of gain at once. Such efforts are made, or at least talked about, in connection with all manner of problems. It is sometimes said, for example, that we should choose new weapons "on a 'maximum effectiveness at minimum cost' basis." [9] Or consider the following criterion, which allegedly guided one military operation: "The Germans' triumphant campaign . . . was inspired by the idea of . . . achieving the unexpected in direction, time, and method, preceded by the fullest possible distraction and followed by the quickest possible exploitation along the line of least resistance to the deepest possible range." [10] In connection with civil-government choices (in India), even the London *Economist* slips. "Above all, in choosing between possible schemes, the Indian planners never admit to using the simple test: which will be more profitable? Which, in other words, will give the maximum increase in the national income for the minimum use of real resources?" [11]

Actually, of course, it is impossible to choose that policy which simultaneously maximizes gain and minimizes cost, because there is no such policy. To be sure, in a comparison of policies A and B, it may turn out occasionally that A yields greater gain, yet costs less, than B. But A will not also yield more and cost less than all other policies C through Z; and A will therefore not maximize yield while minimizing cost. Maximum gain is infinitely large, and minimum cost is zero. Seek the policy which has that outcome, and you will not find it.

It may seem that proposals to use such tests are harmless, since it is impossible to use such a criterion when the analyst buckles down to the comparison of specific alternatives. Nonetheless, this type of criterion error should be taken seriously, for it can lead to some wild compromise criteria. If a person approaches a problem with the intention of using such a criterion, he is confused to begin with; then, when he finds that it will not work, he may fasten upon *any* sort of constraint on gain or cost that converts this impossible test into a feasible one.

9 "Organizing for the Technological War," a staff study, *Air Force*, December 1957, p. 44.

10 B. H. Liddell Hart, *Strategy*, Frederick A. Praeger, Inc., New York, 1954, p. 240.

11 *The Economist*, July 30, 1955, p. 400.

Overlooking Absolute Size of Gain or Cost

One common procedure is to pick that policy which has the highest ratio of "effectiveness," or achievement-of-objective, to cost. In that case, the maximizing of this ratio is the criterion. Note that the terms "effectiveness" and "achievement of objectives" mean positive gains, or the achievement of tasks that it is desirable to carry out. To examine this criterion, let us look at the comparison of alternative military weapons. These could be anything from various antitank weapons to different bombers, but suppose it is the latter. Let the ability to destroy targets, in the relevant circumstances, be the measure of effectiveness. Suppose next that a B–29 system, already on hand and relatively easy to maintain, would be able to destroy 10 targets and would entail extra costs of $1 billion—a ratio of 10 to 1—while System X would destroy 200 targets and cost $50 billion—a ratio of 4 to 1. Does it follow that we should choose the B–29 system, the one with the higher ratio? The answer is surely No, for it might merely be a system that would invite and lose a war inexpensively. To maximize the *ratio* of effectiveness to cost may be a plausible criterion at first glance, but it allows the absolute magnitude of the achievement or the cost to roam at will. Surely it would be a mistake to tempt the decision-maker to ignore the absolute amount of damage that the bombing system could do.

Without constraints on either total level of effectiveness or total budget, the ratio of the two may point to extreme solutions, to nearly-zero or to almost infinite effectiveness and cost. Of course, common sense and empty pocketbooks prevent us from paying attention to such a ratio at the extremes. But what is its significance in the middle-ground that is not ruled out by common sense? Does the ratio take on meaning in these circumstances? The absurdity of the choice to which the ratio might lead is then bounded, and perhaps the chances that its prescription will coincide with the "correct" choice are increased, simply because the ratio is partly penned up. But still the ratio does not take on real meaning. In fact, the only way to know what such a ratio really means is to tighten the constraint until either a single budget or particular degree of effectiveness is specified. And at that juncture, the ratio reduces itself to the test of maximum effectiveness for a given budget, or a specified effectiveness at minimum cost, and might better have been put that way at the outset.

Of course, if the ratios did not alter with changes in the scale of achievement (or cost), the higher ratio would indicate the preferred system, no matter what the scale. That is, if the ratio of achievement to cost were 10 to 1 for the B–29 system and 4 to 1 for System X at *all* levels of achievement, then the B–29 system would be "dominant." For it would destroy 500 targets at the $50 billion level of cost, clearly a better performance than that of System X. But to assume that such ratios are constant is inadmissible some of the time and hazardous the rest. In the bomber illustration the assumption of constant ratios would obviously be wrong, because with larger scales of activity, it would be necessary to buy more B–29's instead of merely using the ones on hand. Moreover, whatever one's belief about the constancy of the ratio, the straightforward test of maximum effectiveness for a given budget (or, alternatively, minimum cost of achieving a specified level of effectiveness) reveals just as much as the ratio—and seems much less likely to mislead the unwary.[12]

It might be observed that ratios are sometimes handy devices for ranking a list of possible actions when (1) the scale of activity is fixed, and (2) the actions are not interdependent (more on this point later). Thus the rate of return on stocks and bonds (the ratio of annual net return to the cost of the investment) is a convenient aid in ranking securities. Then, *with a fixed investment fund,* the set of securities that yields the greatest return for that fund can be quickly determined. Note, however, the limited conditions under which this procedure can be used.

Setting Wrong Size of Gain or Cost

As just suggested, a criterion in which the budget or level of effectiveness is specified has the virtue of being aboveboard. The test's limitation, the fact that it relates to a particular level of cost or achievement, is perceivable with the naked eye. This fact indicates, though, that while avoidance of ratio tests is a step in the right direction, our troubles are not over. For if an incorrect or irrelevant scale of gain or cost is taken as given, the test is unlikely to result in good policy decisions.

In choosing the bombing system, let us suppose that the test is minimum cost of achieving the ability to destroy 10 targets. In these circumstances, the hypothetical B–29 system is better than System X. On the other hand, if the criterion is minimum cost of achieving an ability to destroy 200 targets, System X is better.

---

[12] For examples of ratios used as criteria, see Charles Kittel, "The Nature and Development of Operations Research," *Science*, February 7, 1947, pp. 152–53. For more on the hazards of using ratios as criteria, see Charles Hitch, "Suboptimization in Operations Problems," *Journal of the Operations Research Society of America*, May 1953, pp. 94–95 and *passim*. See also Charles Hitch, "Economics and Military Operations Research," *Review of Economics and Statistics*, August 1958, pp. 199–209.

Clearly it makes a difference which scale of gain (that is, effectiveness) is stipulated, and it would be possible to fix upon the wrong scale.

If the analyst has been instructed to specify a particular level of effectiveness, then someone else has, in effect, chosen this aspect of his criterion for him—for better or worse. If he has leeway, however, and chooses the scale uncritically, he is using what was described earlier as the requirements approach.[13] In other words, he is picking the desired task or level of achievement without inquiry into the sacrifices of other achievements that would be entailed. What he can do to choose the right scale will be discussed a little later. The thing to be noted here is that this sort of criterion error is always a threat in piecemeal analysis.

There is precisely the same danger if the cost (or budget, or resources) is to be stipulated instead of the task. Of course, if the budget is already definitely set by higher level decision, the analysis has to take the predetermined amount as given. But budgets for future years are never "definitely set" in a democracy, and if the analysis is concerned with development or procurement, it is usually the magnitude of future budgets that is relevant. Wherever the budget is subject to change, perhaps on the advice of the analyst, his test should not take as given a budget that is uncritically assumed or stipulated.

Neglecting Spillovers

In economics, impacts of one firm's action upon other firms' gains or costs are referred to as "external economies and diseconomies."[14] For example, an oil well that forces brine into the underground water supply may reduce the fertility of adjacent farmlands. Within firms or governmental units, similarly, the action of one department may affect the gains or costs of operations in other departments. (This would be the case, for instance, if the oil-producing firm owned the farmlands.) The term "spillovers"[15] will be used here, chiefly because it is short, as a general title covering all such effects.

In comparing alternative military policies, it is easy to adopt a criterion that leads to the neglect of spillover effects. For example,

---

[13] Of course, he will presumably minimize the cost of satisfying the requirement—which is, as we have seen, better than choosing uncritically both the task and the method of accomplishing it (the "pure" requirements approach, undefined by any cost considerations).

[14] Or sometimes "divergences between private and social product or cost."

[15] The term "spillover costs" and a helpful discussion of those that arise from congestion are contained in J. M. Buchanan's article, "The Pricing of Highway Services," *National Tax Journal*, June 1952, pp. 97–106.

a classic piece of military operations research may have ignored some impacts on activities other than the one that was directly under examination. In this frequently cited example of successful analysis, alternative arrangements for washing and rinsing mess-kits were compared. As his test of preferredness, the analyst used the minimization of the number of man-hours required to do the job, given a total of four tubs. The optimal arrangement, according to this test, turned out to be the use of three tubs for washing and one tub for rinsing. A hypothetical reaction of the mess sergeant has been reported as follows:

> Yeah, I remember that guy. He had some screwball idea that the mission of the Army was to eliminate waiting lines. Actually I had it all figured out that two was the right number of rinse tubs. With everyone rinsing in one tub the bacteria count would get way past the critical level. But we switched to one rinse tub while he was around because the old man says he's an important scientist or something and we got to humor him. Had damn near a third of the outfit out with the bellyache before we got the character off the reservation. Then we quick switched to three rinse tubs and really made a nice line. "Nothing like a good line to get the men's legs in condition," the old man says.[16]

The purpose of this example is not to disparage this particular piece of analysis, which may have been quite useful. The point is simply to suggest how easy it is, in the comparison of *any* policies, to neglect spillover effects.

Using Wrong Concepts of Cost or Gain

The manner in which cost and gain are defined may seem to be a matter of measurement. These definitions are pertinent in a discussion of criterion errors, however, because wrong concepts of cost and gain may grow out of, or be inextricably bound up with, the adoption of incorrect criteria.

Probably the most important cause of error of this sort is the exclusion of relevant costs from the computation. The costs to be compared are the full system costs of each alternative—all the costs directly or indirectly stemming from the decision. Thus, if we are trying to decide between a missile and an aircraft to accomplish a given mission, it can be completely misleading to compare the manufacturing costs of the competing major equipments. We must also count the costs (except where they are already "sunk") of all the auxiliary equipment, of the ground-handling and support equip-

---

[16] From A. M. Mood's Review of P. M. Morse and C. E. Kimball, *Methods of Operations Research*, in the *Journal of the Operations Research Society of America*, November 1953, p. 307.

ment, of the training of personnel, and of operation for some appropriate period of time.

Our major emphasis in this volume is on peacetime preparations for war and on deterring war. This means that we are interested *mainly* in peacetime, not wartime costs. We are trying to make the most of the resources available for national security in peacetime. In principle, the wartime costs are relevant. In practice, we can frequently ignore them. For in the case of general nuclear war, we expect the war to be fought with the forces in being at its outbreak. The major economic problem is to maximize the capability of these forces by using resources efficiently before the war starts—so efficiently that we hope an enemy will never dare start it. In the case of limited war there may well be significant production of weapons and expenditure of resources after the limited war begins (as in the case of Korea), but occasional wars for limited objectives will cost little compared with the year-in year-out costs of peacetime preparedness. It is estimated that the "cost of United States forces in Korea over and above the normal cost of such forces if no action was taking place" was approximately five billion dollars in the fiscal year 1951/52, about 11 per cent of total United States expenditures for major national security programs that year.[17]

Right and wrong concepts of cost and gain can, however, be illustrated by either wartime or peacetime studies. For example, in a World War II study of alternative ways to destroy enemy shipping, the criterion adopted was the ratio of enemy ships sunk (the gain) to allied man-years of effort (the cost).[18] Now our concern in this section is not with the hazards of such a ratio test,[19] but rather with the nature of these concepts of gain and cost.

Neglect of higher level gain. First, "ships sunk" as a measure of gain may have been an unfortunate choice (whether made by the analysts or by "higher authority"), for shipping could be effectively destroyed by actions such as mine-laying without necessarily sinking many ships. The criterion adopted would have prejudiced the case against such measures.

Neglect of valuable inputs. Next, let us examine the costs of these ship-sinking operations. Costs are the consequences that have nega-

---

17 *Mutual Security Act of 1952*, Hearings before the Committee on Foreign Affairs, House of Representatives, 82nd Congress, 2nd Session, U.S. Government Printing Office, Washington, D.C., 1952, p. 359.

18 Kittel, p. 152.

19 The operation that maximized the *ratio* of ships sunk to allied effort might be a trivial operation sinking one ship or a gigantic effort destroying vast quantities of shipping and requiring the bulk of our resources. There is little assurance that the operation picked solely on the basis of this *ratio* would contribute the most toward victory.

tive values, or in other words they are the sacrifices that have to be made in order to conduct the operation. In the above-mentioned study, man-years of effort—which included those used in construction of vessels and equipment, training, operations, and replacements—appear to be a somewhat dubious measure of these sacrifices. One reason is that man-years, while important in wartime (and in peacetime), were not the only items given up. Thus a method of destroying enemy shipping that used comparatively little manpower, even though it required extremely valuable equipment and skills, had a spurious advantage over a method that utilized relatively worthless equipment and much labor. In effect the test ignored inputs other than man-years as if they were free.

In extreme cases, this sort of procedure may be the correct one. Since the cost of one course of action is whatever has to be sacrificed, that cost depends upon what alternatives are genuinely possible. If, for example, the only courses of action that can be considered are different ways for unskilled laborers to use given equipment to carry out a specified task, the only input that has other uses is the labor. The analysis becomes a time-and-motion study, and a suitable test is the achievement of the specified task with the minimum expenditure of man-hours.

In general, however, the use of man-hours, a "critical material," or any other single input to represent cost is likely to be wrong. Other valuable inputs are usually involved. To ignore these other inputs is to pretend that their use involves no sacrifice, whatever the quantity employed. Another plausible procedure—putting a specific constraint on the amount of each input that is to be used—is in most cases equally misleading. Such a constraint pretends that we do not have the choice of acquiring extra amounts of the input. Sometimes the choices open to us are limited in this fashion, but placing specific constraints on all inputs usually shortens the list of alternatives that is truly admissible; hence it distorts the sacrifices entailed by taking the actions that are in fact examined.

What, then, is the right way to measure cost? The answer, in principle, is that the measures in any particular problem should approximate the value of the alternatives that must be sacrificed. In long-run problems (most development and many procurement choices) the almost unlimited possibilities of substitution in the economy make dollar costs—the dollars representing general resources—a satisfactory measure in most cases, and far superior to such practical alternatives as man-hours. Dollars do, even if imperfectly, take account of the value in other uses of different skills and of factors of production other than labor. In short-run and intermediate-run problems the difficulties are greater, and one must usually impose cost or resource constraints of several kinds. In the extreme case of a field commander who has to prepare for an imminent battle with what he has on hand, the amount of each specific resource (men, tanks, ammunition, and so on) he has is fixed,[20] and no more of any one can be secured at any price. In this case each resource must be taken as a constraint on his tactics. In less extreme cases some resources will be fixed and others variable —the latter frequently at "increasing costs" reflecting either higher incremental production costs in the short run or the withdrawal of the additional resources from increasingly valuable uses elsewhere.

The Navy, for example, may have a certain number of warships readily available for an operation in the Mediterranean (those on station there). In a very short-run problem, no more could be made available from anywhere. In an intermediate-run problem, additional ships could be obtained, but only by the very expensive method of "de-mothballing" or by transferring to the Mediterranean ships whose "outputs" are valuable in other areas (increasingly valuable the more are transferred). In a long-run problem, of course, additional ships could be procured for more dollars. Finding satisfactory cost measures and resource constraints in the intermediate-run problems will frequently tax the ingenuity of the analyst. He must try to avoid treating as free those resources that have value in other uses, or as fixed those resources that, at some cost, are variable. (Also, of course, he should avoid the opposite errors.) While perfection is unattainable, the avoidance of the grosser fallacies is not.

"Sunk" costs and salvage values. Consider once again the costs counted in the search for the best way to destroy enemy shipping. These costs included man-years of effort used in the construction of ships, equipment, and submarines—many of which were already built and on hand. Yet the sacrifice entailed by the use of existing equipment was really its value in other operations,[21] not the original or historical cost of constructing it. Only future sacrifices are relevant—not past. In an economic calculus "bygones are forever bygones."

---

[20] Though even here some of his resources may have value for later battles—a relevant alternative use.

[21] This may well be hard to measure quantitatively, but better the roughest approximation of the relevant magnitude than the most precise measure of the irrelevant.

This point was critical in the comparison that we made above of B–29 and X bombing systems, where the B–29's had already been produced and the X-bombers had not. Should the Air Force "be fair" to System X and insist upon costing each bomber from scratch? Never could considerations of equity be more misplaced. Any real cost associated with the production of the B–29's had already been incurred and is unaffected by what is done with them; if they have no alternative use and no scrap value, then the cost of incorporating them into the bombing system is zero. If they have a scrap value or a value in alternative uses that is sacrificed, then that value is the relevant cost. It is only the extra or incremental cost, not historical or "from scratch" cost, entailed by each alternative system that is relevant to the comparison. The analogy with a business firm's view of cost is complete: in deciding whether to replace an old machine with a new one, the production cost or purchase price of the new machine enters into the calculus, but only the scrap value (or alternative use value) of the old machine, however unfair this may appear to be to the new machine.[22] Considerations of fairness, which might be appropriate in courts of equity, are an undependable basis for choosing production methods or weapon systems.

Frequently in comparing the costs and gains from alternative weapon systems during some relevant period, it will be apparent that some of the systems will be worth more than others at the end of the period. An estimate of the worth of the system at the end of the period—its probable contribution to security in following periods—is commonly referred to as the system's "salvage value." If salvage values are substantial and vary significantly from system to system, they should be subtracted from system costs (or added to system gains). If these values are small or appear to be similar for all systems, of course they can be ignored.

Allocation of Joint Costs

In sub-optimizing, the analyst is frequently confronted with the necessity of computing the cost of X, when some or all of the costs of X are also costs of Y and Z. Suppose, for example, that the construction of an airbase is being considered for joint tenancy by three fighter squadrons and various Military Air Transport Service (MATS) facilities and services. Suppose that the total cost of the base is 100, of which 50 is the cost of basic or common facilities,

---

[22] For examples in which business management formally compares alternative policies in terms of incremental costs and gains, see Horace C. Levinson, "Experiences in Commercial Operations Research," *Journal of the Operations Research Society of America*, August 1953, pp. 220–239.

30 the cost of facilities required by MATS only (these might include, for example, costs of extending or strengthening runways for heavier MATS planes), and 20 the cost of facilities required by the fighter squadrons. If the base were used only by MATS its cost would be 80; if only by fighters, 70.

One way to approach the problem (it turns out to be a treacherous way) is to ask: How should the common costs be allocated among the various uses? One cabinet officer attempted to answer the question in this manner: "The Department believes that the costs of multiple-purpose . . . projects should be allocated on a basis which properly recognizes the added costs of including each separable function and a *fair* [23] share of the joint costs." [24] Again we have the unwarranted intrusion of ethical concepts into an economic calculus. In the Twentieth Century, it appears, we must be fair not only to people, but to weapon systems, machinery, and airbases.

If we keep firmly in mind the principle that only the *incremental* costs for which a system is responsible should be counted, problems of the type presented by the airbase offer no great difficulty. Of course which costs *are* incremental depends upon the breadth of context and the precise definition of the system. If the problem is whether to construct the airbase, and if so, whether for joint tenancy, for MATS only, or for the fighters only, we have to cost the base in three alternative systems. In the first (joint tenancy), the cost is 100; in the second (MATS only), 80; in the third (fighters only), 70. The base should be constructed if its value to MATS exceeds 80, if its value to the fighter command exceeds 70, *or if its value to both combined exceeds 100*. If its value to both combined exceeds 100, the base should be constructed for joint tenancy as long as its value to MATS exceeds 30 and its value to the fighter command 20. A businessman launching a multiproduct investment would think along precisely these same lines in maximizing his profits.[25] As long as the use values can be calculated,[26] the analyst can find a unique solution to his problem without allocating, "fairly" or otherwise, the common costs. The question simply doesn't arise.

---

[23] Italics ours.

[24] Former Secretary of Agriculture Brannan in *Study of Civil Works*, Part 2, Hearings before the Subcommittee to Study Civil Works of the Committee on Public Works, House of Representatives, 82nd Congress, 2nd Session, U.S. Government Printing Office, Washington, 1952, p. 198.

[25] George J. Stigler, *The Theory of Price*, Macmillan Co., New York, 1946, p. 307.

[26] Of course if the use values can't be calculated, the analyst may have a difficult problem on his hands and may have to be content with a "good" or "better" rather than a unique optimal solution. But allocating the common costs won't help him in this case. His fundamental difficulty is his inability to measure military worth.

If a formula for allocating total costs among uses is intended to show how costs respond when one use is eliminated, it can serve a very useful purpose; it is then an attempt to get better estimates of incremental costs. But a formula that is supposed to hand out "fair shares" of joint costs, the shares exactly exhausting the total, is not needed for good decisions and can lead to bad ones. Inability to allocate *all* costs meaningfully among joint products is often a fact of life, not a disgrace or a sign of laziness. The extra cost of adding on a function or a feature can be calculated, or the total cost of the combination of features—but not a meaningful total cost for one feature when undertaken jointly with the others.

APPROPRIATE CRITERIA

So much for potential errors in the devising of tests for preferred policies. What of a constructive nature can be said about the selection of criteria? Clearly, there is no all-purpose criterion, for the appropriate test depends upon what alternatives are open to the decision-maker, upon what aspects of the situation must be taken as given, and even upon what kind of measurements are feasible. Nonetheless a few general observations about suitable criterion-forms can be made.

Maximum Gains-Minus-Costs

If gains and costs can be measured in the same unit, then to maximize gains-minus-costs is certainly an acceptable criterion-form—the equivalent of making the most out of whatever actions can be taken. Suppose the possible courses of action are to put available resources to one of three uses, to be called A, B, and C. Now the gains that could have been obtained by using the resources in B and C are what have to be given up when we use the resources in A. These sacrifices are the *costs* of devoting the inputs to use A, the costs of obtaining the gains from A. When costs are viewed in this way (that is, as gains that must be given up), it is easy to see that maximizing gains-minus-costs is the same as maximizing total gains. If A yields 100 units of gain, B yields 75 units, and C 50 units, A is the use that maximizes gains-minus-costs (100 minus 75), and it is the use that yields the greatest total gain in the circumstances. Note again that this sort of test is possible only when gains and costs are commensurable. It can be used in the comparison of the actions of business firms and certain government measures but only exceptionally in the analysis of military activities.

Either Gain or Cost Fixed

In any situation there are constraints. The decision-maker can borrow additional funds only at higher rates of interest, only a limited number of practical actions are open to him, and there are only twenty-four hours in his day. In many analyses, one constraint is that a particular scale of gain or cost is fixed. This constraint may be imposed when gain and cost are commensurable, as in the case of a firm comparing different ways to use a given investment budget. And it should be imposed, as a rule, for analysis in which costs and gains are incommensurable. In the latter case, naturally it is impossible to maximize gains-minus-costs; what would be the meaning of the ability to destroy ten targets minus one billion dollars? The next-best procedure [27] is to "set" either the costs or gains, seeking the way to get the most for a given cost, or to achieve a specified objective at least cost.

These two criterion-forms are equivalent, if the size of either gain or cost is the same in the two tests. If the test of maximum gain for a $5 budget points to the policy which yields a gain of 10 units, then the test of minimum cost to achieve a fixed gain of 10 will point to the same policy—the one which achieves the gain of 10 at a cost of $5. The two tests also yield equivalent information if calculations are carried out for many different scales of cost and gain. The choice between these two criteria depends largely upon convenience of analysis and upon whether it is gain or cost that can be fixed with the greater degree of "correctness." In some cases it will be immediately apparent which way round the criterion should be stated and the analysis made. For example, the field commander (or his operations analyst), preparing for an imminent battle with a multiplicity of fixed specific resources, will obviously fix the level of resource constraints and attempt to maximize his chances of winning, rather than set some arbitrary chance of winning and calculate the combinations of resources necessary to achieve it. In other cases the preferred way round will not be apparent, and it may indeed make little difference from any point of view which is selected. For example, we can either choose some index of strategic capability we think we might be able to achieve, and calculate the necessary budget, or assume some practical budget and calculate the corresponding index of capability.

This leads us to the big question: How does one determine the right achievement or budget? If the achievement or budget is set

---

[27] Equivalent to maximizing gains-minus-costs in the special case where gains and costs are commensurate and the right level of gains or costs is fixed.

uncritically, the procedure degenerates into the "requirements approach." For example, it might be taken as given that we "need" in the case of a bombing system, a capability of destroying ten thousand targets; and the analysis would seek the cheapest way to achieve that "requirement." What can be done to improve upon this approach?

As a starter, several tasks or scales of effectiveness can be tried, and several budget-sizes can be assumed. If the same system is preferred for all tasks or budgets, that system is dominant. In the bombing-system example, the best bomber (though not the right scale or capability) is then determined.[28] If the same course of action is not dominant, the use of several tasks or budgets is nevertheless an essential step, because it provides vital information to the decision-maker.

Note, however, that the decision-maker, if he is making a quantitative decision or if the qualitative answers vary in the scale, must then himself select the scale of the task or budget. He is presumably helped in reaching this decision by the information about the cost of achieving different tasks or the potential achievements with different budgets. But he has to draw on further information in order to set the right task or budget. He has to ask what task or budget, as the case may be, is consistent with higher-level criteria. Is a capability of destroying ten thousand targets too much or too little in view of the over-all aims of the defense program?

Clearly the analyst will be more helpful if he can answer these questions than if he merely estimates the results for a variety of budgets or tasks. As a matter of fact, he must try to answer these questions approximately if he is even to hit upon a reasonable range of tasks or budgets. He cannot experiment with all possible scales of achievement or cost, as the computations would be too expensive and voluminous to provide any net assistance. Hence the analyst can and should do more than try several tasks or budgets (the procedure which was labeled a "starter"). He should make some inquiry into higher level criteria and into their relationship to possible lower level tests. He may even convert the analysis into a higher level sub-optimization. At *some* higher level, of course, the criterion must be taken as given—that is, to carry out the higher level task at minimum cost, or to get the most out of the higher level budget. But this acceptance of a task or budget as given at some high level is skies apart from setting "requirements" uncritically all the way up and down the line.

---

[28] This may be the decision-maker's current problem—*which* bomber to develop or procure. The decision regarding numbers may be made (and re-made) much later.

Criteria for Deterrence

Suppose that our problem (in 1959) is the design of a strategic offensive force for the middle 1960's to deter prospective enemies from attacking us. Deterrence of World War III is a frequently stated national objective. Our strategic offense force, while not the only force important for deterrence, is generally recognized to be the principal one. But "deterrence" is an elusive and qualitative concept, not too far removed from "military worth" itself. To calculate the relative contributions of alternative weapon systems, base locations, and strategies to deterrence, we require a much more precise and objective proximate criterion. What is a good criterion—one that avoids the pitfalls we have outlined and is consistent with the high level national objective of deterrence? Let us consider some possibilities (all of which have been used in similar studies), beginning with some that, while avoiding the crudest fallacies, are still clearly unsatisfactory.

a. *Numbers or weight of offensive weapons (for a given budget).* Criteria of this general type are used in a surprisingly large number of cases by military correspondents, columnists, and other "experts" who should know better. Our deterrent force is held to be effective because we have more (or bigger) bombers than the Russians; or thought not to be effective because the Russians allegedly are building more long-range missiles than we. Little thought is required to dismiss such crude counting devices. What matters is not the number of aircraft or missiles on either side, or any other physical measure of their size, but in some sense the damage they are able to inflict. A missile that can carry a small bomb and deliver it within 10 miles of its target presents nothing like the deterrent threat of a missile that can carry a large bomb and deliver it within two miles.

b. *The number or value of enemy targets that can be destroyed (for a given budget).* This is a criterion that makes a little more sense. It takes into account not only the numbers of our offense bombers and missiles, but also their operational effectiveness, the yield of the bombs they can carry, their ability to penetrate enemy defenses, and the accuracy with which their bombs can be delivered. It is still, of course, an ambiguous criterion, and requires more precise definition. For example, what target system—population, industry, or military bases—should we use to keep score on alternative United States strategic forces? In principle, the one whose prospective destruction would be most likely to deter the Russians from striking. If we are not sure which target system would have this characteristic, we might have to try several, to see whether the same strategic force performed best (or well) against all. Similarly, what kind of air defenses should we assume the Russians will have in the mid-sixties? Here we will almost certainly have to assume several kinds and quantities to test the alternative forces, giving the Russians some opportunity in each instance to adjust their defenses to the composition and basing of our force. But there remains another ambiguity in this criterion —one of crucial importance. Should we count the destruction potential of the entire force (the customary procedure) or the potential of that part of the force that survives an enemy attack? In other words, are we interested in a "strike-first" or a "strike-second" capability? Which is consistent with the national objective of deterrence?

To the extent that we are concerned with deterring a direct Russian assault on us, the essence of deterrence is a strike-second capability. The Russians will be deterred, not by the damage we can do if they refrain from attacking, but by the damage we can do if and after they attack. An American force that can make a devastating first strike but is easily destroyed on the ground is more likely to invite direct attack than to deter it. (It may, however, have some utility in deterring lesser aggression, for example, against third parties.)

c. *The value of enemy targets that can be destroyed (for a given budget) after an enemy first strike.* This is much closer to what we want. It requires us, in allocating our given budget, to reduce the vulnerability of our force whenever money spent on reducing vulnerability (say, on dispersal, on increased alertness, or on underground construction) will increase our strike-second capability more than the same money spent on additional bombers or missiles and the personnel to operate them. In general, this is what deterrence demands. This criterion is probably good enough to justify extensive quantitative comparisons of our capabilities with different kinds of weapons (bombers and missiles), different base systems (continental United States *versus* overseas *versus* on or under the seas; fixed *versus* mobile), and different modes of protection (such as ground alert, airborne alert, dispersal, and underground construction). In making the comparisons we must consider a range of possible Russian attacks, with special emphasis on those that look most dangerous to us, and are therefore most likely to be preferred by the Russians.

But we should be under no illusions that this good, workable criterion is good enough to yield definitive answers. It too ignores several vital elements of this exceedingly difficult and complex problem. For example, it ignores the danger that World War III might break out as the result of an accident or misunderstanding; it would do us little good to deter a rational enemy from attacking only to stumble into hostilities by accident (and some weapons and modes of operating them are more "accident prone" than others). This criterion partly neglects the objective of deterring "minor" aggressions, such as enemy attacks on United States or free-world positions in the NATO area or the Middle East. A strike-second capability would also have a strike-first potential, but it is not obvious that the measures that are optimal for deterring a direct attack are also optimal for deterring an indirect one. This test also ignores a good many interdependencies among different military capabilities: can our strategic offensive forces be designed in such a way as to contribute to our ability to fight limited, local wars or to facilitate the task of air defense? Can it even be assumed that the best force for deterring World War III is also best for fighting it—in the event that deterrence fails?

There is, moreover, the problem of what size the "given" budget should be. The optimal mix of weapons, bases, and protective measures may or may not be similar at different budget levels (this could be tested by trying a number of different levels). But even if the mixes are similar, it is tremendously important to get the absolute level somewhere near right—to have a deterrent force that is good enough, not merely the best achievable on a budget too low to provide deterrence, or one so good that we over-deter World War III and have little left over for other vital capabilities. The fixing of this level requires, of course, a higher level study that focuses on the size of the national security budget and its allocation among the major military claimants—for strategic offense, strategic defense, limited war, and cold war. While rigorous maximization at this level is silly, hard straight thinking in an economic framework can help, and can be helped by quantitative calculations. The size of the budget for the strategic offensive force must not be accepted *uncritically* as "given"; its determination is one of the most important national security decisions.

365-417 O - 69 - 9

VII

INCOMMENSURABLES, UNCERTAINTY, AND THE ENEMY

We have seen that at best the problem of determining relevant, correct criteria is troublesome. The complications that are now to be introduced make the problem still less tractable, and indeed affect the very meaning that must be attached to the word criterion.

INCOMMENSURABLES: MEANING, EXAMPLES, AND TREATMENT

Incommensurables, as we use the term, are certain consequences of the alternatives compared—those consequences that cannot readily be translated into the common denominator or denominators that are being used.[1] Thus, if gains are being measured in dollars (as they ordinarily are in a business problem), the effects that cannot be measured in money by any objective and generally acceptable method are incommensurables. In principle, these effects are not different from any others. They may or may not be measurable in their own appropriate quantitative terms, in a manner helpful to the decision-maker. (If not, they are "intangible" as well as incommensurable.) Moreover, an *individual* can compare them subjectively with the other effects. Indeed, implicitly the decision-maker does translate these incommensurables into the common denominator when he makes a choice. But they cannot be expressed in terms of the principal or common unit in any *generally acceptable* manner. Of course if no single unit is used extensively enough to be regarded as a common denominator, there is no basis for distinguishing between effects that are commensurable and those that are not. This is often the case in consumers' research, which we regard as the most rudimentary, least ambitious type of economic calculus.

Incommensurable objectives and costs are likely to mar the neatness of any analysis, whether it pertains to problems of business,

---

[1] We saw in Chapter V that it is possible to carry out a quantitative analysis with two or more objectives or common denominators as long as we are satisfied with a set of "efficient" solutions rather than an optimal solution. We will usually assume in this section that a single common denominator is used in the explicit calculus. But see pp. 147–148, below.

the military, other parts of the government, or individual consumers. No matter how industriously the analyst works at devising a single quantitative test, considerations that must be measured in other units (if at all) will still be pertinent to the final decision. It is difficult to find problems of military choice in which such considerations do not have to be given serious attention. We have already seen[2] that in high level military problems incommensurables may severely restrict the usefulness of quantitative analysis. They are likely to dominate any analysis of the optimum size of military budget, or its division among the military services.

Even at relatively low levels incommensurables are likely to be too important to ignore; and in some low level problems they are dominant. In other words, there are military problems at all levels in which a definitive economic calculus cannot be made because of the multiplicity, incommensurability, or nonmeasurability of the objectives or costs.

Consider the importance of such effects in military problems where quantitative analysis can be helpful. In many such problems, cost can be fairly satisfactorily measured in dollars, and the objective as the degree of achievement of some military mission. But suppose that the preferred (that is, minimum-cost) method of achieving the objective is expected to involve the loss of more lives than some alternative method that is more expensive in dollars—even when the costs of recruiting and training the additional personnel required are included, as of course they should be, in the calculations. There are at least two reasons we might be concerned about this. First, the higher casualties *may* affect the morale of our forces and degrade their efficiency in a manner not taken into account in the calculations, making the efficiency of the first method less than it appears on paper. In *principle* such reactions should be taken into account explicitly; in practice, the intangible character of a factor like morale may make this impossible. Second, we are interested in lives for their own sake. We want to win a war with no more casualties than necessary. Fewness of casualties *per se* is an objective in planning any military operation, even if a subordinate one, that is not fully allowed for by including the resource cost of replacements.

Other examples of incommensurables frequently encountered in military problems include the whole gamut of other factors influencing morale; increased capability to fight a war of type B when the major consideration is the capability to fight war A;

---

[2] Chapter V.

impetus to specially promising state-of-the-art advances in choosing the next generation of some type of equipment; the maintenance of a "healthy" aircraft industry or broad mobilization base in selecting contractors (and therefore weapons) ; repercussions of all sorts on United States foreign relations and hence foreign policy (an extreme example is action that a potential enemy might regard as "provocative") ; the effects of some methods of winning a war on the prospects for a tolerable and durable peace.

There are several ways of handling incommensurables in quantitative analysis. One way is just to ignore them: if there is no objective way to make them commensurate, have no truck with them at all. This method is not recommended; the significance of the numbers in an analysis depends upon the importance of effects not encompassed by those numbers, and the recognition of this dependence should not be left to chance. What effects are finally measured in terms of the common denominator must be made clear;[3] what major effects are *not* so measured, though perhaps initially considered as candidates for inclusion, should *at least* be described.

Sometimes it is suggested that, if the analyst works hard enough, *everything* can be put in terms of the common unit. For example, it has been suggested that the saving of a human life can be priced by consulting (1) the values implied by past decisions, (2) the average court award, or legal compensation, for accidental death, (3) the value of a person as productive capital in the economy— the sum of his expected future net earnings discounted to the present, or (4) the cost of saving a life by the cheapest alternative method. Now any of these devices may be useful in particular problems, but none provides a generally valid and appropriate measure of "the" value of human life, and the real meaning of some of them, in the absence of an organized market (like a slave market) to which governments and individuals adjust their actions, is hard to unravel.

It is possible, in some cases, to estimate the values attached to human lives implied in some World War II decisions—the amounts that were in effect traded for lives; but these values differed from one situation to the next and were not necessarily the values that should then have been, or ought now to be, assigned to lives. Court awards provide no generally appropriate value; they are notoriously influenced by adventitious factors. As for the value of a man as a productive resource, it does not reveal our valuation of a life

---

[3] For example, was the performance of the system degraded to reflect high casualty rates or not?

as such. Besides, the value of a person as peacetime productive capital is almost irrelevant in war, when we are willing to sacrifice peacetime values to achieve war objectives. The costs of saving additional lives by other methods may suggest a maximum value in some circumstances, or may be useful in suggesting a reallocation of budget among various policies designed to save lives. It is inefficient, in the technical sense, to spend $10 million per life saved in the design of a bomber system when we can save lives for a small fraction of this by, say, installing seat belts in ground vehicles. Of course people may attach different worths (apart from the diverse values of persons as productive resources) to different lives—those of children, older people, military personnel, civilians, volunteers, or persons who die in particularly brutal or painful ways. But this fact simply reinforces the original proposition, that there is no *generally acceptable* method of valuing human lives.

Suppose that the analyst's problem is the comparison of alternative strategic bombing systems that are to be maintained in a state-of-readiness to deter attack. Some of these systems will, it is estimated, result in higher casualties among crews if and when war occurs. The analyst includes in the cost of each system the expenses of recruiting and training the additional personnel required because of these higher casualties. He also estimates the degradation of each system resulting from high casualty rates. Should he *in addition* include some valuation of the crew lives lost as human lives in his cost calculations? Almost certainly not. In the first place, in an exchange of bombs, the crew lives lost will inevitably be swamped by the lives of civilians and allies lost to enemy attack: if our interest is in lives *per se,* it would be ludicrous to value the dozens in the air and neglect the millions on the ground.[4] In the second place, we are really interested not in the lives lost in any particular operation, but in the war. If we prejudice victory by selecting relatively inefficient (costly) systems because they save lives in a particular operation, we may well prolong the war and lose more lives before we win it, or even lose the war itself.

This is not to say that the attempt to "price" lives in all problems is unhelpful. Nor is it to say that it is hopeless to try to value other effects which appear at first glance to be incommensurables. In specific analyses ingenuity can often go a long way toward measuring such effects in terms of the common unit. We cannot say just

---

[4] The expected destruction of life and property on the ground incidental to the campaign is an important incommensurable which certainly should influence the choice of weapons or strategies.

where to draw the line between effects that should be measured in terms of the common denominator and those that should not. We can say, however, that insistence on the measurement of all effects in terms of a single common unit will not make for the most useful analysis. A Congressional committee was probably justified in concluding its review of an evaluation of federal resource development projects: "Some of the effort to place monetary values on indirect benefits is nothing short of ludicrous." [5]

The analyst is then frequently left, after the prudent exercise of his ingenuity in reducing everything to a common measure, with one or more important effects that defy reduction. We call them "incommensurables." What can the analyst do about them that will be helpful either to himself in making recommendations based on his study, or to the decision-makers directly?

(1) A device that is frequently useful where there are two or more objectives, each of which is measurable but with no common unit of measure, is the calculation of the set of efficient solutions as explained earlier in our chapter on "Efficiency in Military Decisions." This may be enough in itself to identify some system that is preferred to an existing or proposed system—a good practical aim for quantitative analysis. Furthermore, by limiting the alternatives, a calculation of this kind can facilitate the exercise of judgment in selecting, from among the efficient solutions, a near-optimal one.

(2) It will frequently be possible to calculate the value one must assign the incommensurable either in dollars or in terms of the unit measuring the major objective if he is to prefer System A over System B. Thus, the analyst can tell the decision-maker: Bombing System A will give you a target destruction potential of 1,000. If you are willing to take the diplomatic trouble and risks involved in various overseas countries, System B will provide the same potential for $1 billion less (or will increase the potential to 1,500 for the same budget). For System A to be preferred, one must put a value of at least $1 billion on the avoidance of the trouble and risk. Someone must exercise judgment in deciding, but it can be helpful in making this decision to know that $1 billion is at stake rather than $100 million or $10 billion. [6]

---

[5] It is ludicrous by our test of *general acceptability*. Each individual Congressman can decide, for example, how many millions the development of the Northwest region at the expense of the rest of the country is worth to him, but there is no reason to expect the valuations of Congressmen from Oregon and Oklahoma to coincide.

[6] If all the leading alternatives involve significant and different incommensurables, this device is not very useful. The situation would then be like that in which the little boy valued his puppy at $50,000 and, according to his story, sold it for that amount. How? By accepting a couple of $25,000 cats as payment.

The calculation of such break-even points or trade-offs is more difficult than, but far preferable to, the common practice of placing limiting constraints on the solution. For example, instead of trying to calculate the impact of casualty rates (through morale) on crew performance, a frequent practice is simply to rule out all solutions in which casualty rates exceed a certain arbitrary percentage. Or to take another example, some political problems of overseas basing can be swept under the rug, as far as the analysis is concerned, by simply declaring certain countries off-bounds, or by specifying in advance an "intercontinental" solution. Some such constraints on an analysis are necessary and justified. Limitations of time and cost alone prevent the consideration of every conceivable alternative and opportunity. But the selection of constraints must be made with care and discrimination and with knowledge of the havoc they can play with the analysis. Casually selected or arbitrary constraints can easily increase system cost or degrade system performance many-fold, and lead to solutions that would be unacceptable to the person who set the constraints in the first instance if he understood their implications.[7]

(3) In some cases where systems achieve incommensurable objectives, the analyst may be able to design another system which is better at achieving some things and as good, or almost as good, at achieving the others. Suppose for example that he is comparing the capability of a force based overseas in peacetime with that of a mobile force based in the Zone of the Interior (ZI). Suppose that quantitative analysis shows the ZI force to be markedly superior, but that the stationing of troops overseas is believed to be important for the maintenance or strengthening of our alliances. The analyst may be able to design and suggest a third solution, say, a rotation system, which has most of the advantages of the ZI based force without this incommensurable though important disadvantage. The rotation system may be almost as effective (for a given budget) as the ZI based force, and almost as acceptable to allies, while perhaps having some advantages (realistic practice in mobility) possessed by neither of the original alternatives.[8] In many cases the analyst's ingenuity may be more rewardingly exercised in trying to find ways of satisfying multiple objectives than in

---

[7] We know of studies in which an arbitrary limitation on casualties led to solutions in which, at the margin, $100 million was being spent to save a single life. Even if one regards a human life as "worth" this much, the same amount of money could be spent in ways to save many more.

[8] If the new system is better in *all* respects than any of the alternative systems it is said to be "dominant." Pure dominance is almost always unattainable, but it provides a goal for systems invention which may be approximated.

devising common measures for them. It can in fact be argued that the *chief* gain from systematic analysis is the stimulus that it provides for the invention of better systems.

(4) Finally, as a minimum, the incommensurables can be displayed and talked about. Quantitative or qualitative information about them may be helpful to decision-makers.[9] Although by definition they are not commensurable with the other costs and gains, clues to their impact can often be given. A very short essay on the possibilities of negotiating base rights in India might be sufficient to rule out certain alternatives that look attractive in the quantitative analysis. The annoyance to the population of sonic booms cannot be subtracted from fighter defense kill potential, but it will still be helpful to present estimates of the numbers of such booms over populated areas with different basing systems or training concepts. Such effects can be partially traced out, sometimes quantitatively, after the fashion of consumers' research, and presented in an exhibit that supplements the principal estimates. This can be helpful to the decision-maker in the same manner that consumers' research is helpful to the consumer.

UNCERTAINTY

The estimates of costs and gains considered so far are average, predicted, or "expected" outcomes. But we know in advance that, for all sorts of reasons, these amounts may be off the mark. Actual costs of development or production of new weapons never precisely coincide with advance estimates and sometimes differ from them by factors of two to twenty. Times of availability are also very hard to estimate accurately, and as a rule greater uncertainty attaches to estimates of effects or gains than to estimates of cost and availability. The enemy never does what we expect; indeed, he always has greater or less capability than we expect. Every war is full of surprise outcomes. Now while uncertainties of these sorts are pervasive, they are likely to affect some systems in a comparison more than others. The availability of the overseas base system is more uncertain than that of the ZI base system. We can predict the performance of a weapon of which we have a prototype with much greater confidence than the performance of a rival weapon on the drawing board. As a consequence, Systems A and B may offer identical predicted outcomes, yet differ greatly with respect to other possible outcomes. These differences may be a matter of some moment if, say, A's possible results are all thought to be

---

[9] For pure "intangibles" the information would have to be qualitative.

nearly the same as predicted, but B's range from fabulous success to utter disaster. Yet while such differences in the pattern of uncertainty—or, more precisely, in the "frequency distribution of outcomes"—are matters of great concern, it is ordinarily impossible to attach a value or price to them. A price, that is, which would have any *general* acceptability. In some situations and for some persons, to reduce the chance of a bad outcome is worth a great deal. In other situations or for other persons, even a small chance of an extremely favorable outcome carries a high premium.

Types of Uncertainty

It may help to put this complication in proper perspective if we see how pervasive uncertainty is. Perhaps this will also help show that uncertainty is inherent in the nature of things and is not necessarily evidence of lazy or careless estimation. One can sympathize with the general who shouts at his analyst: "Give me a number, not a range": unique numbers are easier to work with and to think about than ranges or probability distributions. But he is probably asking his analyst to falsify the real world in a manner that will make it impossible for him, as a commander, to make good decisions.

Uncertainty about planning and cost factors. Every model uses as inputs certain relations between its elements which are known in the military as "planning factors"—for example, the number of miles a unit can march or drive in a day over specified terrain; the radius of destruction of atomic (or other) weapons of specified power against specified objects; the circular probable error (CEP)[10] of bombing with a given bombsight as a function of, say, speed and altitude; the average number of hours a cargo plane can be used per day. It is apparent that we may attempt from time to time to determine some planning factor, for example, CEP, as a function of bomber speed and altitude, or of other parts of the system. In that case the particular planning factor would be a variable, not a given, in the analysis. But in any particular analysis many planning factors must simply be taken as given; there is never time to calculate everything from scratch. So they are borrowed from other analyses of varying quality, from books of official planning factors assembled and published by the military Services, or from other sources.

This procedure may conceal uncertainties that arise for two reasons: first, the quality of the sources from which the factors

---

[10] The radius of the circle within which half the bombs will fall.

are borrowed varies from fair to bad to biased (they have seldom been estimated with the particular requirements of this analysis in mind) ; and second, they are almost invariably "numbers" rather than ranges or probability distributions, suppressing significant variations in the behavior of the relations in the real world.[11] Divisions do not always march the same number of miles in a day, even over "specified" terrain, for any of a thousand reasons. Even if one has the right *average* value of CEP (almost certainly an unwarranted assumption), it will be wrong for any particular strike.

Factors used to estimate costs of specified military forces and weapons systems are always uncertain, especially when they relate to the distant future. Cost estimating is an approximate art even in the most well-run businesses. Wages and material prices are subject to unforeseeable fluctuations. More important, it is impossible to predict accurately how many men, what kinds of material, and how much time will have to be paid for. On production items the range of error in cost estimates may be only 10 per cent or so—perhaps too small to be worth bothering about in view of other uncertainties inherent in the analysis. But the actual costs of developing, producing, and operating complete weapon systems have frequently exceeded cost estimates made prior to development by factors of ten or more, largely because of the technological uncertainty that existed when the costs were estimated. Necessary modifications that double system cost must be regarded as fairly normal.

Uncertainty about strategic context. Every war, whether all-out, limited, or cold, is fought in some "strategic context"—at a certain time and place, with certain enemies and allies, to achieve certain political objectives. Since the ranking of alternative forces or weapon systems may depend decisively upon the strategic context, the analyst must make assumptions about it.

In some circumstances (during a war, or in planning for an imminent outbreak of war at a particular place against a known enemy), there may be a fairly obvious "best" set of assumptions to make about the strategic context. Analysts working on North Atlantic convoy problems during World War II knew where and when the war was occurring, who the enemy was, who our allies were, the constraints under which both sides were operating, and the general political objectives and grand strategy of our side.

---

[11] We are arguing *not* that the use of average values is necessarily wrong, but that the uncertainty this covers up should be recognized.

But when the problem is to choose military forces in peacetime that will give us a capability of fighting future wars, good assumptions about the strategic context may be far from obvious.

Consider the questions that have to be answered about the strategic context in choosing among alternative future bombing systems. First, when will war occur? System A may seem far preferable if the threat is in 1960, system B if the date is 1965. Who will be our enemies and allies? The answer is always less obvious than it seems—if a few years are to elapse (how many could have guessed in 1942, or even in 1947, that Germany and Japan would be among our most valued allies in 1957?). Will our allies make overseas bases available for our bombers, or will they yield to "atomic blackmail"? Will the war be general or local, all-out or limited? What constraints will be imposed—say territorially, as in Korea, or on the use of nuclear weapons? It is apparent that the "best" bombing force will depend critically upon answers to questions of this kind.[12] And, curiously but perhaps fortunately, there is no *authoritative* way for the analyst to get the right answers—or any answers. Of course no single military service can provide answers; decisions about war and peace (and kind of war) are made at the highest level of the government—our own and the enemy's. And just as no Congress can make decisions binding our future Congresses, neither can a President or Joint Chiefs of Staff effectively bind a future President or Joint Chiefs.[13] The analyst must face up to gross uncertainties of this strategic sort, and his recommendations may well depend upon the way he does so.

Technological uncertainty. Technological uncertainty may occasionally be serious in the analysis of current operational problems, but as we try to peer further and further into the future it becomes more and more important and can, indeed, dominate the analysis. Technological uncertainty is the central problem in research and development decisions. There is always some technological uncertainty connected with research and development; otherwise it would not be research and development but production. But because of the interdependence of all factors in an analysis, this kind of uncertainty may influence analyses that are not focused on research and development.

---

[12] It is also apparent that the strategic context will in turn be affected by the forces and weapon systems we choose. Enemies will attempt to force us into the kind of engagements for which we are not prepared. If we prepare only for hot wars, they may choose to defeat us in cold ones.

[13] Except in a negative way. If certain forces having long lead times have not been provided, future Joint Chiefs will not be able to fight certain kinds of wars in certain ways—even if one of them then appears to be in the nation's interest.

For example, uncertainty regarding the A-bomb importantly (and properly) influenced our preparations for the final stages of our campaign against Japan in World War II. Uncertainty about the H-bomb—whether it would work, how soon, and how cheaply—affected not only the nuclear and missile development programs [14] but our strategic concepts and plans for future military forces of all types. Uncertainty about the progress of various missile programs is now (1959) grossly influencing not only missile development but bomb development, aircraft development, aircraft procurement, the composition of our air defense forces, and plans for civil defense. Expert guesses about the dates of operational readiness of important missile systems vary by as much as a decade: no one can be sure which guess is right.

Uncertainty about the enemy and his reactions. Two kinds of uncertainty stem from the fact that the object of military forces is to oppose other military forces—those of enemy (or potentially enemy) countries. A military tactic, strategy, force, or development program is never good-in-itself, but only good-in-relation-to the tactics, strategy, forces, and future weapon systems of an enemy.

First, our factual "intelligence" about an enemy is always less than perfect, and when the enemy country is a dictatorship that ruthlessly and efficiently suppresses information and restricts travel, our ignorance of its military capabilities may be gross. The practice of military intelligence agencies of presenting numbers ("best guesses") rather than ranges in their estimates obscures but does nothing to remedy the incompleteness and unreliability of most of the information on which the estimates are based. As is characteristic of uncertainty, the probable errors of intelligence estimates increase as we look further into the future. How can *we* predict when a Russian missile system will be ready when we know that the Russians, with far more knowledge of their program than we have, cannot make such a prediction with any accuracy themselves? It is unfortunate that our choice of weapon systems usually depends as critically upon enemy parameters as upon our own.

Second, and even more fundamental than our ignorance of his capabilities, is our ignorance of the enemy's "intentions" (in the vocabulary of the intelligence agencies) or "strategy" (in the language of the theory of games). Military forces are used, wars

---

[14] It is widely reported that the intercontinental ballistic missile development program suffered from lack of support in the early years because the guidance problems seemed so intractable. Then the unexpected development of the H-bomb made even very inaccurate ICBM's useful.

are fought, against human beings exercising human intelligence. The best way for us to fight a war, or to prepare to fight one, is likely to depend decisively upon decisions that have been or will be made in, for example, the Kremlin. But no one has ever devised a good method of predicting the decisions of other human beings —even of human beings with whose psychological conditioning and drives we are fairly familiar. With what confidence can we expect the men in the Kremlin to be "deterred" by promises of "massive retaliation"? In what circumstances would they, or anyone else, start a thermonuclear war? What kinds of limitations (for example, territorial or in the use of nuclear weapons) might we be able to impose upon them in limited wars? What are their territorial targets likely to be in cold and limited wars? If they start a war, will they rely on mass or surprise attack (our "best" defense is likely to be very different in the two cases)?

It is easy to spend billions preparing for a kind of war or strategy that the enemy would never choose. Some individuals have special insight into the behavior of the Russian (and other) élites, but it is difficult enough to tell in advance which ones really have insight and which merely have confidence—let alone to assess the confidence that we can place in their predictions.

Statistical uncertainty. Finally, there is "statistical" uncertainty, the uncertainty resulting from the *chance* element in recurring events. This is the kind of uncertainty that would persist even if we could predict enemy strategies and the central values of all important parameters. We know that if we flip a penny a thousand times, it will come down "heads" approximately half the time; but that if we flip it only ten, the proportion of heads may be much higher or much lower. Similarly, we may have a radar sensing system that we expect to identify enemy planes 90 per cent of the time; it will still be possible for the planes to slip through undetected on the one day that counts. In most long-range problems, statistical uncertainties are the least of our worries; they are swamped by uncertainties regarding central values and states of the world. In some problems, however, we cannot rely exclusively on average or expected values.

The Treatment of Uncertainty

What can the analyst do to take account of the proliferation of uncertainties resulting from our ignorance of the future? As with incommensurables, the most important advice is: Don't ignore them.[15] To base an analysis and decision on some single set of best guesses could be disastrous. For example, suppose that there is uncertainty about ten factors (such as, will overseas bases be available? Will the enemy have interceptors effective at 60,000 feet?) and we make a best guess on all ten. If the probability that each best guess is right is 60 per cent (a very high batting average for best guesses from most sources), the probability that *all ten* are right is one-half of one per cent. If we confined the analysis to this best-guess case, we would be ignoring a set of futures with a 99.5 per cent probability of occurring.

So we must design the analysis to reflect the major uncertainties, and this usually means computing results for a number (sometimes a large number) of contingencies. If overseas bases may or may not be available, and some of our systems depend upon them more than others, we must test the systems assuming we have them, and again assuming we do not. If future missile CEP's (that is, accuracies) are grossly uncertain, we must make the computations with at least a high and a low value, and possibly one or two intermediate ones. If our strategic bombers may be required in local wars in the Middle East or Far East as well as for general war, we must test them in all theaters and circumstances that appear likely and important.

The trouble with computing "all interesting contingencies" is a practical one. The number of cases to analyze and compute increases as the power of the factors that are permitted to vary.[16] Unless discretion is used in restricting the cases to combinations that are really significant, we are likely to formulate a problem that is too big to solve—or at least too costly or time consuming to be worth solving. Developments in high-speed electronic computers in recent years are making it possible to compute solutions to more and more complex problems. Nevertheless it is still necessary to cut problems down to manageable size on computational grounds alone, and usually far more important is the effort required on the part of the analyst to assemble the data and structure the models for each of numerous cases. Testing systems in a different kind of war or even a different theater may double the

---

[15] Ignoring uncertainties is a chronic disease of military planners and analysts. There is a great temptation and frequently great pressure to use official planning factors, official intelligence estimates, and the best guesses of higher military authorities.

[16] As noted earlier, if there are two uncertain factors (say, kind of war and CEP) and each is permitted to take four values, the number of cases is only 4^2 or 16. But if ten uncertain factors are permitted to take four values each, the number of cases soars to 4^{10}, which is over 1,000,000.

work of analysis—and therefore either the manpower or the time required to complete the study.

So the practical problem is to design the analysis to reflect the truly significant contingencies but, in order to keep it manageable, only these. This requires practical judgment of a high order; the analyst must know a great deal about his problem—in effect, what is likely to be important and what unimportant in influencing the solution—before he structures it. Sometimes he can cut down on the number of cases that have to be computed by constructing an *a fortiori* argument; that is, if he is lucky as well as skillful, he may be able to show that his preferred system is best (or better than some alternative) when he makes unfavorable assumptions regarding many of the uncertainties, and therefore does not have to bother with computations involving favorable assumptions. But at best he will have to show how things can be expected to turn out under a number of different future circumstances, and usually one of his systems will look best in some contingencies, another in others. How does the analyst then choose the preferred system? What decision does he recommend?

Making Decisions in the Face of Uncertainty

Suppose that we are considering the choice of an anti-ICBM system and are weighing the relative merits of three proposals—1, 2 and 3—in what appear to be the three most interesting contingencies—A, B and C (see below). Contingency A is very favorable to the United States—perhaps the contingency in which we

Illustrative Payoff Matrix

System	Contingency		
	A	B	C
1	100	20	0
2	60	40	0
3	20	10	10

strike first against the enemy's offensive force, so that its attack on us is disrupted and our defenses against it are fully alerted. Contingency B is much less favorable; here the enemy starts with a massive, coordinated attack. Finally, C is a catastrophic contingency—one, say, in which the enemy discovers a way to make a simultaneous attack without any warning against all our defended targets. We "score" the three systems for performance in each contingency by the utility or worth of what is left—100 representing everything, and zero representing nothing.

System 1 is obviously a fair-weather system, which works splendidly if everything is just right, but is almost worthless when the going is rough. In particular, it is easily saturated. System 2, on the other hand, while leaky, is not rate-of-fire limited, and does almost as well (or badly) in case B as in case A. Both 1 and 2 are useless against a C attack. System 3 is a desperate sort of system, which uses all the funds available for burrowing underground. In consequence, even the light attack assumed in A practically destroys the country, while even the heavy, warningless attack of C leaves a little to rise from the ashes.

Which of these three systems do we choose if our choice really is restricted to these three? There is no completely satisfactory and generally accepted theory either of how people *do* make such choices or of how they *should* make such choices.

Maximize expected value. If it is possible to estimate the utilities (that is, the worths) of the various outcomes (as we assumed in the above table), and *if* we can also, at least roughly, calculate the probability of each contingency, it would appear reasonable to choose that course of action or system that maximized expected utility.[17] Thus, in our example, if we attached equal probability to the three contingencies, we should choose system 1. If we believed B to be four times as likely as A, and C to be wholly unlikely, we should choose system 2.

This principle is, within limits, a valid and useful guide in some situations. While attaching utilities and probabilities to outcomes is difficult, we can frequently do it in a rough fashion—yet well enough to narrow the field of choice to good alternatives. Of course there may not be agreement about the utilities and probabilities of the various outcomes. The customer may insist that the analyst let him make his own estimates and draw his own conclusion. But the theory directs our attention to the relevant questions.

Minimax. There is, however, an important circumstance in which it is inappropriate to ask questions about the probability of outcomes. If the contingency depends not upon "nature" or luck but upon the choice of a malevolent enemy, we are not concerned with probabilities. The rational man, it is argued, should assume that the enemy will do his worst and therefore choose the system

---

[17] L. J. Savage, *The Foundations of Statistics,* John Wiley and Sons, New York, 1954, pp. 1–104 (chapters 1–5).

that will minimize the maximum (worst) the enemy can do.[18] The shorthand expression "minimax" can be used to refer to this strategy. If in our example we assume that the enemy can choose the contingency, it appears that he would choose C, and that the "best" we can do in consequence is to opt for system 3 and guarantee ourselves a survival utility of 10.

There is much in this view that is relevant and important in the analysis of military problems. Where the enemy controls the choice, it is not meaningful to compute probabilities. We should focus our attention instead, as this view does, on the freedom of the enemy to choose, and the likelihood that he will choose something pretty unpleasant, if not the worst. Moreover, the enemy's worst —or "reasonable" worst—is a case on which the analyst should concentrate—not exclusively but heavily. Wishful or lazy thinking too often causes the analyst to dwell on threats that he thinks we can counter, rather than the more dangerous ones that will appeal to the enemy.

Nevertheless, these concepts and rules borrowed from game theory must be applied to actual military problems with a good deal of discretion. War, especially of the modern nuclear variety, is not a two-person zero-sum game; that is, a game in which only two players are involved, the gain of one being exactly equal to the loss of the other. And it is only in such a two-person zero-sum game that even a very intelligent enemy can "reasonably" be expected to choose the course that is worst for us. In non-zero-sum games, what is best for the enemy is not necessarily what is worst for us. To take an extreme case (although not very extreme any longer) : if the enemy has an end-of-the-world machine, the worst thing he can do to us is to use it, but this also happens to be the worst—not the best—from his point of view too. We would be foolish to adapt our whole strategy to this contingency, which will have little appeal to him.

In much less extreme cases minimax (as we are using this term) is unduly conservative. If we choose our systems solely for their ability to shore up our defense in the worst case, (a) we may not be able to shore it up enough to matter much (as in contingency C in the example), and (b) we may be sacrificing oppor-

---

[18] The term "minimax" and the general flavor of this argument are borrowed from the theory of games, but we are *not* using the term minimax in the technical sense in which it is used in the theory of games. We are thinking of situations in which we have to choose a system in advance, and the enemy knows of our choice. The classical work on games is John von Neumann and Oskar Morgenstern, *Theory of Games and Economic Behavior*, Princeton University Press, Princeton, N.J., 1944 (2d ed., 1947). For a brief and highly readable volume, see J. D. Williams, *The Compleat Strategyst*, McGraw-Hill Book Co., Inc., New York, 1954.

tunities for major improvements in our capabilities to deal with other contingencies that have some substantial likelihood of occurring. For even if the situation approximates a two-person zero-sum game, the enemy may not act as game theory assumes. A minimax solution is motivated by the idea that the enemy is completely rational, perfectly intelligent, can read minds, never makes mistakes, and so on. Enemies, especially enemy countries, are seldom like that. They are run by bureaucracies that make mistakes like our own. Their intelligence has blind spots. Their leaders are full of prejudices. There is a vast amount of irrational inertia in the determination of policy. Probably no great military leader in history except the conservative Ulysses S. Grant ever worked on minimax assumptions, and Grant had such superiority in resources that he could afford to be (it made sense for him to be) conservative. Great profit can be derived in many circumstances from anticipating enemy mistakes and being prepared to take advantage of them. Minimax forfeits such opportunities.

Any departure from the two-person zero-sum assumptions accentuates the conservative bias of the solution. The contingencies in this kind of analysis are seldom under the complete control of the enemy. In our example the enemy can obviously influence who strikes first, but he can no more decide it than we can (he can decide to strike first, but that is a different matter: we may learn of the decision and preempt him). Nor can the enemy simply will the massive, simultaneous warningless strike that we feared could be so devastating in contingency C. He can will a research and development program in the hope that such a capability will prove feasible; but nature will determine whether the program is a success. In mixed cases of this sort, and *a fortiori* where there is no game at all (that is, where the only "other player" is "nature," as when the uncertainty is statistical), the bias of a solution that assumes a malevolent intelligence at work may be extreme.[19]

So we are left with no generally satisfactory answer. *If* we can estimate the probabilities and the utilities of outcomes even roughly, as sometimes in "playing against nature," expected value seems satisfactory; but if we have to use physical outcomes in lieu of their utilities, or are confronted by an intelligent enemy, we must beware of a bias toward recklessness in applying this technique. *If* circumstances approximate those assumed in the two-

---

[19] Some find more intuitive appeal in a variant of the minimax solution variously called minimizing the maximum "regret" or "loss." It at least gives less conservative solutions in many instances (including our example, where it would opt, not too convincingly, for system 1 !). See L. J. Savage, pp. 163–171.

person zero-sum game, we can compute the minimax solution, keeping in mind its conservative bias.[20]

This reference to conservative and reckless biases in various solutions provides some clue to the basic difficulty in generalizing about the behavior of rational men in the face of uncertainty. For while rational men do act in the face of uncertainty, they act differently. There are audacious commanders like Napoleon, and conservative ones like Grant—both successful in the right circumstances. Different people simply take different views of risks—in their own lives and as decision-makers for the nation. Some "insure" and others "gamble." It is therefore most important, whether the analyst calculates a general solution or not, that he present responsible decision-makers with the kind of information provided in the example on p. 136, and let them use their own risk-preferences in making the final choice. The risk-preferences of responsible decision-makers may be very different from those of the analyst.

Designing for Contingencies

But the most important part of the answer to the pervasive uncertainty facing the analyst or the military planner is not greater subtlety in making difficult choices, but *the design of systems to cope with more of the critical contingencies*.[21] A situation like that represented in our example, where each of three proposed systems is good in one contingency and bad in the others, covering only one best, should be a challenge to the analyst and the decision-maker to invent a better system—one that looks good in more than one contingency. Truly dominant systems—those that are better in all circumstances—are hard to find, and require luck, too, but it is rare that a resourceful analyst cannot get closer to dominance than the systems in the example.

The first thing to try in designing a system capable of coping with several contingencies is to mix ideas, concepts, or hardware from the systems designed for each contingency. Mixed systems usually involve extra costs, which can be estimated, but are frequently worth it (we have rarely relied on pure weapon systems). Multiplicity is more frequently justified in development than in procurement and operations (both because uncertainties are greater at the development stage and because the extra costs of mixing or "duplicating" are less). In other cases mere mixing may

---

[20] In some circumstances, e.g., if the intelligent opposition aspect is unimportant but we cannot estimate probabilities, we may want to minimize the maximum regret.

[21] In this respect the problem of dealing with uncertainty is like that of dealing with incommensurables.

be an inadequate or inferior solution. It may be better, for example, to redesign the hardware to serve more than one purpose, combining some of the characteristics of the special purpose hardware previously compared. Or drastic redesign of operational concepts, or the invention of new ones, may be indicated. Protection against warningless attack, for example, may be better secured by concealing some of our targets, or making them mobile, than by burrowing underground. Or there may be superior concepts for burrowing. Whatever the device, the analyst's responsibility is to come up if he can with a system that has no critical soft spots and that still looks very good in the favorable contingencies.

Sometimes the redesign of systems will have a different objective from dominance. Suppose that an apparently dominant system—one that is best against some contingencies and as good as its rivals against the others—is still alarmingly ineffective in the most probable situation. Suppose, in other words, that it is still only the best of a bad lot as far as the principal contingency is concerned. We may wish in this instance to invent a system that is better against this contingency even if it is worse in other less probable situations.

Thus one reason for inventing new alternatives is to find a dominant one, enabling us to choose regardless of the probabilities that particular contingencies will occur. Another reason may be to improve upon the present poor set of alternatives.

Hedging and Insurance

Despite the ingenuity of the analyst, there may remain in an otherwise preferred system some chance of an extremely unfavorable outcome. Sometimes the best he can do (a very useful best) is to calculate the least-cost method of providing some hedge or insurance (complete or more usually partial) against this contingency. This is necessary information for a rational decision whether or not the hedge is worth making.

Hedging in busines operations is frequently a highly organized activity supporting special markets. Hedging is also a typical reaction to uncertainty by individuals. A family planning an automobile trip may buy a new set of tires even though it estimates the chance of a blowout as less than 50 percent. A hedge against even a slight possibility of a fatal accident (or major inconvenience) may be worth the price. Any purchase of insurance is an example of hedging.

The military does not have a futures market in which it can hedge, nor can it eliminate uncertainty by the purchase of insurance from commercial companies. But there are innumerable ways in which it can hedge against loss or disaster, and analysis can define and cost them. Mixed systems can be regarded as one kind of hedge; general purpose systems, another. A hedge against ECM (electronic counter-measures) may be some kind of electronic *counter* counter-measure. The extra cost can be computed in money and resources, or in the degradation of performance in more favorable contingencies.

It is not necessary that the hedge be complete and certain in its operation. We may, indeed, be able to deter the enemy from taking certain actions by what are called "low-confidence" measures—measures with only a moderate (50 percent or less) chance of succeeding. If the enemy action is one that he would not undertake without high confidence, we can sometimes deny him this confidence by a cheap low-confidence measure of our own (if its chances of success are only 30 percent, the enemy's cannot be higher than 70 percent). There are occasions when intermittent patrols make sense—for the military as well as for the police. Fair-weather fighters may be useful even in defense: the enemy may be unable to plan an attack for a time when bad weather is predicted, or the weather may turn out to be good in spite of the predictions of enemy weather forecasters. Low-confidence measures are no general substitute for high-confidence measures, but they are useful hedges in some circumstances—when they are cheap and we have reason to think that the enemy is likely to insist on high confidence from his standpoint.

Reducing Uncertainty

Sometimes an important, or even the most important, conclusion of the analyst is that measures should be taken to reduce some of the uncertainties and that some decisions should be postponed until more is known with confidence.

Knowing when to make decisions may be as important as knowing what decision to make. The costs and dangers of "indecisiveness," of postponing decisions too long, are obvious and widely appreciated. But there are also costs and dangers in making decisions on the basis of incomplete and uncertain information. In recent years we have wasted billions by making premature decisions to produce operational equipment with trivial improvements in capability, when what was needed was a broad program of research and development to buy knowledge of markedly improved hardware. We simply did not know how to design equipment with a capability that would be worth the high costs.

So if the question is what to procure, the best answer may be: nothing but a research and development program, or a test program, at this stage. Do not try to decide until you know more, until you know enough about costs and performance to make useful cost-effectiveness studies. This does not mean doing nothing. One important job of the analyst is to spot the critical areas in which more knowledge is needed, and to devise proposals for getting it.

And if the question is what to develop, the answer may well be in terms of a strategy for buying information rather than a detailed blueprint of some futuristic operational weapon. With technological uncertainty layered on top of strategic uncertainty, it is rarely possible to specify an advanced weapon system far in advance and schedule a development program for it. And it may be a mistake to try. The first step is to determine the critical uncertainties and to undertake a research and development program to resolve them. Only then will we be in a position to schedule the next steps.

DEALING WITH THE ENEMY

As we have seen, many of the crucial uncertainties in any military analysis stem from our ignorance of the enemy and his intentions. Analysts make two very common mistakes in dealing with the enemy—the first is to regard him as stupid, inflexible, and devoid of initiative; the second is to attribute to him diabolical cunning, unlimited flexibility, and boundless initiative. In the cliché of the Pentagon, we insist on picturing him as either 2 feet tall or 10 feet tall. The first kind of blunder is the more frequent, but either one can ruin an otherwise excellent analysis.

How much capability and flexibility, for example, should we attribute to the Soviet Union? We have a fairly firm knowledge of her current industrial capacity and output and of her industrial growth rates. But how many ICBM's, or atomic submarines, or nuclear weapons, or defense radars can we expect them to have by 196–? These are important questions. The design, procurement, and deployment of our own weapons are obviously sensitive to the answers.

The first thing to realize is that we do not and cannot know the answers with certainty. No one can. The Russians do not know themselves. We cannot answer similar questions about our own strength in the 1960's. We should not take the best guesses of the intelligence community as gospel. The best guesses may be wrong, and even if right today, the Russian leaders can change their plans and make them wrong tomorrow. Another common error is to assume that the Russians will put all their potential for expansion into the one capability (say, atomic submarines) that happens to be critical to our analysis. The best thing we can do is to project Russian industrial capacity and the Russian military budget—with margins of error—and then face up to the Russian allocation problem in much the same way we face up to our own.

The recognition of the extreme importance of enemy intentions and enemy reactions in most military problems has led to much work in recent years on techniques to improve our ability to predict enemy reactions (that is, reduce the uncertainty from this source) and to deal with them more effectively. The most important of these are (a) game theory, and (b) "gaming"—sometimes called "war gaming" or "operational gaming."

(a) Game theory has contributed a conceptual framework for thinking about situations of conflict that has proved extremely valuable in many problems. The preceding discussion would have been impossible without constant use of concepts derived from the theory of games—like "strategy," "solution," "dominance," and "minimax." Game theory has been effectively applied to a number of tactical problems in which a conflict or "game" occurs repeatedly (as in the case of duels between fighter aircraft). It has also provided useful insights that have aided in the solution of more complex problems. But for broader military problems, formal game theory solutions have two serious deficiencies. First, most military problems are too complex to permit of practical game theory solution (even simple games like checkers are too complex for practical solution by the theory). Second, and more fundamentally, as we have seen, wars are not two-person zero-sum games—and little progress has been made in solving other kinds of games. Two-person means that there are only two sides, each with a consistent and unambiguous set of values: there is no room for "third forces" or for imperfect and shifting coalitions. Zero-sum means that the gain of one side corresponds exactly to the loss of the other; each side is playing the same game with the same rules and the same understanding of the scoring. But in war there may be no "victor"; the total losses may far exceed the total gains; the two sides may fight for objectives that are qualitatively different, not mere mirror images of each other. When the game theory solution is computed for a problem in which the circumstances do not correspond to the two-person zero-sum assumptions, its relevance depends more upon its intuitive appeal to "rational" men than on the rigorous proofs of the theory. The solution is likely, as we have seen, to be an unduly conservative one.

Game theorists have probably concentrated too much, however, on *solving* games. More emphasis should be placed, not on finding formal solutions, but on simply exploring and studying game situations—particularly, of course, those pertaining to non-zero-sum games.[22] New variants on these actions, possible gambits in tacit bargaining, the manner in which specific steps do influence pay-offs, and the probable enemy reactions to specific policies—all these matters deserve intensive study, and game theory is one framework for studying them.

(b) Another means of exploring such questions is experimentation with various gaming techniques. Gaming has almost nothing in common with game theory, which it long antedates. Gaming is an exercise engaged in by human beings (individuals or teams) on two (or occasionally more) "sides"; whereas game theory has so far been a branch of mathematics. Gaming is an extremely flexible device, and can take numerous very dissimilar forms. There are war games that allow great freedom to the participants in making moves, and others that are highly "structured," with rules almost as precise as those of chess.

War games have long been used by military staffs, and were perhaps most highly developed in the nineteenth century by the German General Staff (*Kriegsspiel*). They have been used by the military, however, primarily as training devices, to teach junior officers principles that others have previously learned in actual combat. The possibility of solving problems of strategy by gaming has been considered by military authorities, but usually dismissed as unpromising. Not only is it difficult to reproduce reality adequately on a sand table, but the time and manpower required for a single play of an elaborate war game preclude the numerous plays that are needed to test out several strategies on both sides in various contingencies—the sort of test that could point the way to optimal, or at least good, strategies for blue.[23]

Recent developments have concentrated on speeding up play, a necessary condition for the effective use of gaming as a problem solving device. High-speed computers have been used both to assist players in making moves and to help the umpires trace the consequences of moves.

There is little doubt that the gaming activities of this kind are worthwhile. In particular, there is no doubt at all that the players

---

[22] Thomas C. Schelling, "The Strategy of Conflict: Prospectus for a Reorientation of Game Theory," *Journal of Conflict Resolution,* September 1958, pp. 203–264.

[23] For an historical account see Clayton J. Thomas and Walter L. Deemer, Jr., "The Role of Operational Gaming in Operations Research," *Operations Research,* February 1957, pp. 1–27.

learn from the game, that they acquire insights that are valid and useful to the extent that the game has been well designed. But there is some doubt that games of this kind are very effective as problem-solving devices. Rapidity of play, which permits numerous plays, is a necessary but not a sufficient condition of a game that will solve problems; and the number of plays is, in any event, still grossly inadequate by analytic standards.

Operational gaming has never really solved the criterion problem, and its attempts to evade it by substituting human beings for explicit objectives have merely obscured the issue. Game theory at least faces up to the problem, although its solution, minimax, appears too conservative except in repetitive zero-sum games. Gaming, while it frees itself from this specific and unsatisfactory criterion, has none to take its place. The blue player is usually told to behave as if he were a blue commander or the blue government; the red player, as if he were a real red. The extent to which the players are rightly motivated is unknown and unknowable.

For this and other reasons the results of repeated war games are difficult to interpret in most cases. One knows the outcomes of the plays, but one cannot determine analytically the relative importance in determining the outcomes of (1) the skill of the players, (2) their motivations, (3) the structure of the game, (4) the assumed values of various parameters, and (5) chance elements. One is left essentially with the intuitive insights that the players and observers believe they have derived from playing.

These insights, however, should not be belittled. While less than totally satisfactory (what alternative approach would give results passing this test?), they can be provocative and suggestive of good solutions which can be tested by more analytic methods. It is terribly important, no matter how it is done, to look at things from the enemy's point of view. Games provide a good stimulus and setting for doing so.

The importance of keeping the enemy's viewpoint in mind was brought out earlier in the discussion of criteria for deterrence. Many persons, leaving enemy viewpoints and responses out of account, have assumed that a large offensive force automatically provides deterrence. If we look at the matter from the enemy's point of view, a large *but vulnerable* Western striking force provides *negative* deterrence (at least as far as thermonuclear attack is concerned). In general, the analyst who looks at problems too exclusively from his own country's point of view, like some conventional military planners, is likely to forget how ingenious and resourceful the enemy may be. The war gamer whose force has been destroyed by enemy initiative is much less likely to make this dangerous kind of mistake.

The Meaning of Criteria

Earlier it was convenient to discuss criteria as though the term referred to definitive tests of preferredness. These reflections on incommensurables and uncertainty, however, make it clear that the word "criterion" sometimes means a partial test—one that provides a significant rather than a nonsensical basis for the comparison of policies and yet not a basis that embraces all the relevant considerations. In many problems, the precise relationship between proximate criteria and the ultimate test will not be known, and hence the former must be incomplete tests.

This is true in business as well as in military and other governmental problems. Consider, for example, an attempt by the managers of a firm to apply the test of "maximum profits from available resources." [24] Let us assume that when the managers consider several alternative courses of action, they can predict expected profits, and also something about the variability of profits, under each alternative policy. In other words, they can say to themselves, "Under Policy 1, profits would be $1 million, plus or minus $200,000. Under Policy 2, expected profits would be $2 million, though there is a chance that they might run as high as $3 million or that losses of $1 million would be incurred." What *is* "maximum profit from available resources" in this situation? It may be defined as maximum *average* profit, but in any event, it will be an incomplete criterion, because its relationship to the ultimate test will not be fully traced out. The ultimate criterion is to maximize something—it is usually labeled "utility"—which *depends upon* expected profits, upon the other possible profit figures, and upon the management's attitude toward risk and uncertainty. But the precise nature of this relationship is not ordinarily known. Hence to show which course of action yields maximum expected profit is to compare the policies in terms of one selected policy-consequence, that is, to apply a partial or incomplete criterion. To compare the policies with respect to other possible outcomes or to variability of outcome is to use other incomplete or partial criteria.

In military problems utility has frequently been labeled "military worth." Let us assume, for the moment, that the military

---

[24] See G. Tintner, "The Theory of Choice under Subjective Risk and Uncertainty," *Econometrica*, IX, 1941, pp. 298–304; A. Alchian, "Uncertainty, Evolution, and Economic Theory," *The Journal of Political Economy*, XVIII, June 1950, pp. 211–221, or S. Enke, "On Maximizing Profits," *American Economic Review*, XLI, September 1951, pp. 556–578.

worth we wish to maximize in a particular military problem is a function of the retaliatory power of SAC, the frequency distribution of results, the size of the federal budget, various diplomatic impacts, and the number of lives saved. We do not know how important some of these effects are in relation to others. Consequently we can devise no complete criterion which points to the "correct" force composition of SAC; the determination of such a force involves value judgments by several of the Executive departments and of Congress. However, we can show what would happen to a measure of SAC's retaliatory power with different force compositions. If possible, we should show data related to some of the other effects (for example, the frequency distribution of results). In any event, it is plain that maximum expected offensive power for a given SAC budget is an incomplete test, and it should be understood that the term "criterion," when it is used in connection with the economic analysis of military problems, often refers to such an incomplete test.

VIII

PROBLEMS ASSOCIATED WITH TIME

Much of the discussion so far has had a static dimension. We have usually spoken of costs and of benefits (or achievements or capabilities) as if they were timeless or, perhaps, concurrent. In fact, every cost is incurred and every benefit is realized at a particular point in time, and we are far from indifferent to the dates of these points. In 1960, 1961 seems far more significant to most of us than 1970. In our illustrative example in the fuller text we had to face up to some of the difficulties associated with time because we were dealing with a real problem. We did so in that example by constructing a simple artifice, dividing the relevant future into three periods—Period I, Period II, and "beyond the horizon"—and ignoring time differences within each period. In this chapter we will consider, in a quite general manner, some of the principal difficulties associated with time and some of the methods of dealing with them. We will discover that, as with other difficulties of systematic analysis, simplifications and compromises with the ideal are inevitable, but that there are better and worse ways to simplify.

In any economic analysis we are likely to begin with certain assets inherited from the past. In a business firm these usually include buildings, machinery, and inventories. In the airlift example used they included not only the 400 C–97 cargo aircraft, but airbases, cargo handling equipment, maintenance depots, spare parts, trained crews, and so on. The production or "initial" costs involved in creating these assets have been incurred in the past; they are "sunk" costs[1]—bygones that are irrelevant in any comparison of the economic merits of alternative means of accomplishing future objectives. The use of some of these inherited assets to achieve any particular future objective may involve "opportunity" costs; that is, the use of these assets may make it necessary to forego valuable opportunities of using them to reach

---

[1] Sunk costs and salvage values were also discussed in chapter V. Because of their importance and their pertinence to the treatment of time streams, we review these topics briefly here.

some other future objective. Thus, the 400 C–97's might have some use (after conversion) as tankers to refuel bombers; if they have, their net value as tankers is a legitimate cost—an opportunity cost —of providing airlift. But their value as tankers (if any) bears no necessary relation to their historical cost of production: it could be considerably greater or much less. In our example it was assumed that their marginal value as tankers (or in any other alternative use) was zero. While this may not have been literally true (they would bring something if sold for scrap), it was probably a close enough approximation for the kind of analysis we were making. The alternative-use value of specifically military equipment is frequently (although by no means always) small enough in relation to other costs that the analyst is justified in ignoring it.

The only costs and benefits in which we are interested in economic comparisons of alternatives are future costs and benefits. The opportunity costs associated with using inherited assets are one category of future costs. Far more important, in most cases, are future production costs, installation costs, maintenance costs, and operating costs.[2] These future costs are incurred at different times in the future. Some of the production costs may be incurred this year; some of the operating costs, ten years from now. We may think of the prospective costs associated with any one of the alternative means of achieving a military objective as a stream in time, whose width at any particular moment is proportional to the costs to be incurred at that date. Similarly, we may think of the benefits or capabilities associated with each alternative system as a stream in time, with width proportional to the capability expected on each date.

Now not only are the total *areas* of the cost streams (or benefit streams) associated with different alternatives likely to differ; their shapes are also likely to differ, and significantly. For example, if one compares the cost streams associated with a least-cost fleet and a least-procurement fleet, he may discover that the least-cost stream is broader (that is, costs are greater) in the early years, when new, more efficient equipment is being procured, and narrower in the later years, after it has come into use. The savings in later years more than counterbalance the additional expenditure in the early years if no discount rate is used, that is, if costs incurred in any year are assigned the same weight or significance. But, in principle, this procedure is obviously wrong. The shapes

---

[2] These are also, of course, opportunity costs. All significant economic costs are opportunity costs. The reason production costs, for example, are significant, is that the productive resources used (or used up) could have been used to produce something else of value.

of the streams do matter. We attach greater significance to costs and benefits this year than to prospective costs and benefits in future years, and in general we attach less significance the more distant the future year. In other words, we discount the future.

WHY DISCOUNT?

Individuals, firms, and governments borrow and lend in markets in which interest (or discount) rates are invariably positive. Consider first the individual or firm. If I have control over funds today I can invest them and obtain 3 or 4 percent more every year. To me $100 today is the equivalent of at least $103 or $104 a year from now or perhaps $150 ten years from now. The government is in an analogous position. Tax income today can pay today's bills. Tax income a year from today is less useful. Today's bills must be paid by borrowing at 3 percent (unless the government prints or otherwise creates money), and next year's tax income used to repay the loan plus interest. So $103 next year is the equivalent of $100 this year.

The principal reason interest rates are positive is that control over funds makes possible capital investments (in factories, machinery, inventories, and so on), and capital investment can be productive. This creates a large demand for present funds, and the demanders are willing to pay for the limited supply that is available. Each borrower must be willing at least to match what the marginal borrower is willing to pay. Each saver can get (at least) that price for the use of his funds.[3] As a result, the price for funds measures their opportunity cost or, in the language of economics, the marginal productivity of capital.

At the same time, this rate on funds measures our marginal time preferences—that is, the rate that we are willing to pay for consumption now rather than consumption later. The reason for this is that each person is free to adjust his savings until another dollar spent on current consumption is as important to him as another dollar saved for future consumption. If the prevailing rate of interest is 3 percent, each of us values the marginal dollar put into consumption now as much as $1.03 for consumption next year. If this were not true, additional dollars would be shifted from consumption to savings. Hence the prevailing rate of interest

---

[3] There is no need for any saver to accept less, even though some people would be willing to save and lend to industrial borrowers at lower—even zero—interest rates.

measures the opportunity cost of funds diverted from either consumption or production.

In most instances, there is an additional factor that affects discounting and makes for a whole structure of rates rather than a unique interest rate. This important factor is the risk and uncertainty associated with different ventures. Risky business enterprises must pay much more than the "pure" rate of interest to obtain control of funds—and it is right that they should. If the risky enterprise does not have a prospect of a higher return than the safe one, the funds should go to the safe one. Or, to view the matter in another way, the future net gains (or gains and costs) of risky ventures should be more heavily discounted than the estimated net gains from relatively safe enterprises.

In comparisons of alternative military systems, the reasons for discounting are precisely the same as they are in the private economy. A $150 cost (or gain) that will occur ten years hence is the equivalent of only, say, $100 now, first of all because resources can be made to grow that much if put to alternative uses. A least-cost fleet may use funds *now* which, if we had opted for the least-procurement fleet, could have been used to finance productive private investment. It should be charged at least a rate representing the market's evaluation of the marginal productivity of such investment.

In fact, it should be charged more than this. That market rate is the *minimum* rate appropriate in comparing military systems. There is the second, and in the typical military case quantitatively more important, reason for discounting future costs and benefits, namely, the existence of risk and uncertainty about the gains and costs. First, the war for which we are preparing may occur before the date at which the cost would be incurred or the capability realized. Second (less likely but conceivably), peace might break out, or disarmament be achieved, before the date in question. More generally, all sorts of things can happen that will completely alter the need for forces of the type envisaged, and they are more likely to happen the more distant the year. The future costs and benefits are prospective rather than real, and may never become real. We live in an uncertain world, and its military aspects are more plagued by uncertainty than most others. Military technology is passing through a revolution—apparently an accelerating one. Concepts, tactics, strategies and alliances are all in ferment. Future weapon capabilities that look attractive today may be useless tomorrow.

WHAT RATE?

The straightforward (but not necessarily the easiest or preferred) way to make costs and benefits at different times commensurate is simply to apply an appropriate discount rate to future costs and benefits, so that all are stated in terms of "present value." [4] This is what a business firm does, at least implicitly, in comparing present and future amounts, preparatory to choosing policies that maximize present value.[5] But what is the "appropriate" rate for this discount calculation? In general terms, the rate should be the marginal rate of return that could otherwise be earned—that is, the rate that reflects the productivity of the next-best opportunity. If the investor can borrow and lend freely, the marginal opportunity will turn out to yield approximately the market rate of interest. If he faces a fixed budget, the marginal opportunity may yield some other rate.[6] If legal or other constraints close off certain opportunities, those investments are simply not relevant and have no bearing on the selection of the rate of discount.

It is often argued that governments should not discount future amounts at as high a rate as do individuals and firms, because governments should take a longer-run view and endeavor to provide more for posterity than the decisions of private individuals would provide. We may indeed want governments to take a long view and to make extra provision for later generations—by increasing *total* public investment (in either defense or other forms) or by stimulating private investment. But, having settled this issue, governments should presumably try to channel the investment funds into those activities that have the highest rates of return. Similarly, an individual who wishes to provide more for his heirs should cut his consumption and raise his total investment, but should channel his capital into its most productive uses.

---

[4] The present value of any future cost or benefit is

$$\frac{a_n}{(1 + r_1)(1 + r_2) \cdots (1 + r_i) \cdots (1 + r_n)}$$

where a_n represents the future value in year (or period) n, and r_1, r_2, r_i, r_n the appropriate discount rate during the ith year (or period). If the r's are equal, the present value$=\frac{a_n}{(1 + r)^n}$.

[5] It is usually assumed that businessmen attempt to maximize the present value of anticipated future income streams, costs counting as negative income. Present value maximization is the equivalent in economic dynamics of profit maximization in economic statics.

[6] This brief discussion is greatly oversimplified, but in our judgment, the finer theoretical points do not affect the main conclusions that can be drawn about comparing military systems. For more details and complexities, see Roland N. McKean, *Efficiency in Government through Systems Analysis, With Emphasis on Water Resource Development*, John Wiley and Sons, New York, 1958, pp. 74–95, and Jack Hirshleifer, "On The Theory of Optimal Investment Decision," *Journal of Political Economy*, August 1958, pp. 329–352.

In either instance, this means discounting streams of cost and gain at the marginal rate of return, not at some artificially low rate.

In government, the marginal opportunity depends upon the problem of choice that is being considered. Usually, when we look several years ahead, leaving the resources in the private economy is a pertinent alternative, one that may be taken to be the marginal opportunity. In other words, the government can repay debt or refrain from borrowing or taxing instead of making the purchase under consideration. As a consequence, the rate the government has to pay to borrow funds—on the order of 3 per cent—is a suitable minimum rate. If leaving the resources in the private economy is not an admissible alternative—if the problem is to allocate a given budget—the marginal opportunity and yield may be something else.

As suggested previously, however, we usually have to add an appropriate risk premium to this minimum rate. We should allow to some extent for the chances that the future benefits we expect may never be realized, that the costs may not have to be incurred, and that the estimated amounts may turn out to be wrong. But we do not know and cannot hope to learn precisely how risky any particular military investment is.

Some investments are certainly riskier than others. The probability of war (or peace) breaking out before realization of the anticipated benefit or cost is probably similar for all military systems; but some systems will be more vulnerable than others to uncertainties about technological advances, future strategic situations, and enemy capabilities and intentions. Advanced weapon systems, such as a future hypersonic long range bomber, appear to be among the riskiest enterprises of the modern world. Airlift systems appear to be much less risky. Technological advances in economical air transportation occur more slowly than in offensive and defensive weapon systems, and it seems likely that we will be able to use a lot of economical air transportation for something important through the 1960's even if technological or political developments rule out the danger of limited warfare in the vicinity of Bangdhad.

Perhaps, therefore, an appropriate discount rate (pure interest plus risk premium) for a military investment like that in airlift capacity would be similar to a rough average in private enterprise —say 6 to 8 per cent per annum; while the appropriate rate for an advanced weapon system might be higher—say 10 per cent or more. Twenty per cent would be an extremely high discount rate to use: it reduces a cost or benefit anticipated 5 years hence to almost a third its nominal value, and one anticipated 10 years in the future to about a sixth. If risks are *really* high enough to justify a 20 percent discount rate, investments whose payoffs are in the distant future can rarely be justified unless the nominal payoffs are spectacular.[7] The appropriate discount rate during World War II appeared to be even higher than 20 percent because immediate results were so much more important than distant payoffs; so we required that development and procurement be justified on the basis of payoff during a very short period.

It is pretty clear that a rate as high as 20 or even 15 percent per annum could not be justified in present circumstances (1960) by the probability that war will intervene. If we really thought that war was sufficiently imminent to warrant discount rates of 15 to 20 percent, we would be spending much more than 40 billion dollars annually on military programs. Discount rates as high as these are appropriate only for systems with high risks of obsolescence. Of course *if* our assessment of the probability of war increases, we should both increase military expenditures and use a higher discount rate in choosing *among* alternative purchases.

WHAT VALUE FOR FUTURE INPUTS AND OUTPUTS?

We have said that future gains and costs should be discounted— that distant amounts should be weighted less heavily than present ones. Whatever the prices of individual inputs and outputs, a hundred dollars now is worth more than a hundred dollars ten years from now because (1) it can produce something, or "grow," in the meantime, and (2) we prefer a unit of satisfaction now to one ten years later. All this is not to say, however, that the price or value of *particular* objects will be lower in the future than at present. We may well expect the cost of certain inputs or the value of certain outputs to rise.

Thus, in addition to discounting cost and gain streams, a private investor must also do his best to estimate the future prices of inputs and output. He may reason that the cost of petroleum will be higher in 1970 than in 1965 because the more easily accessible supplies will be exhausted. Or he may expect the worth of an "advertising capability" to go up because of the growth of his competitors. Clearly, the future values of such items and therefore the *undiscounted* amounts of future costs and gains, are ex-

---

[7] Expenditures on research and exploratory development projects, however, which are cheap and may lead to spectacular payoffs in a decade or two, can be justified at 20 percent or even higher discount rates. However, we are not arguing that all uncertainties can or ought to be reflected in discount rates.

tremely important. We must not fancy that proper discounting can make up for their neglect.

Similarly in the comparison of military systems, we should discount future amounts, but the undiscounted gains and costs of certain defense capabilities may be greater in 1970 than in 1965. Careful discounting does not by itself assure that the streams of costs and accomplishments are being handled properly.

This fact becomes especially important when we start taking into account the interdependence between our policies and the enemy's future actions. Suppose that an enemy is expected to have no ballistic missile capability in the early 1960's, a gradually increasing but less than decisive capability until 1965, and, after 1965, the ability to annihilate us if we have no defense. In these circumstances, anti-missile capabilities are clearly worth more to us in 1965 than in 1960. In fact, the appropriate value in the current year is zero—if the enemy cannot attack with missiles and if there are no by-products from an immediate capability like effective training for next year. On the other hand, some anti-missile capability in 1965 and later would be, on this supposition, of enormous value.

Consider a hypothetical comparison of two weapon systems. Suppose that our expected budget for defense against ballistic missiles is "given" during the next few years, and that we want to develop and procure antimissile defense systems that will optimize, in some sense, our capability over time to shoot down incoming missiles. System A, adapted from a system developed primarily for defense against bombers, promises to give us some immediate capability but has little growth potential. System B cannot possibly provide a defense for several years, but promises a comparatively effective defense beginning, say, four years hence when it becomes operational. In choosing between the systems, we must assign reasonable values to capabilities in different years before we discount. Or it might be more practical to reformulate the problem, stipulating a reasonable time-path for our capabilities and discounting only the cost stream to seek the most efficient system for achieving the stipulated capability.

Thus, when we urge the discounting of future amounts, we mean that command over general resources now is worth more than command over the same amount of resources next year—not that specific objects are worth more now than in the future. We emphasize this fact because we do *not* wish to encourage the built-in tendency of governments to undervalue future outputs (see the concluding section of this chapter). To repeat, before discounting streams of cost or gain, one must take pains to assign realistic values to future inputs and outputs.

SOME PRACTICAL DODGES

As a practical matter, we must abstract from some of these complexities. It is impossibly difficult in most comparisons to determine the appropriate future budgetary constraints, the proper list of alternatives and the yield of the marginal opportunity, the degrees of riskiness of various opportunities, and finally the appropriate discount rates. In these matters, as in others, we must simplify reality to a considerable extent. We seek to simplify reality enough to make systematic thought and calculation feasible yet not so much as to make the results inapplicable. Some crude approximations are usually justified, if we are careful to avoid distortion and bias. Needless to say, judgment must enter into this procedure of devising "practical dodges."

The Time Horizon

In comparing alternative weapon systems, it is never practical or desirable to estimate benefits and costs for all eternity and to determine and apply appropriate discount rates to these streams. It is always necessary to cut off the analysis at some point, ignoring or crudely lumping costs and benefits thereafter. Our ability to foresee the future becomes so limited after, say, ten or fifteen years, that for purposes of comparing weapon systems it seldom pays to try. If we did use appropriate discount rates, with appropriate allowance for risks, the comparisons would, in any event, be little affected by the distant years. The simple and straightforward thing to do is to omit them.

If a fairly early date is taken for the time horizon of the analysis, it may be desirable to lump net benefits beyond the horizon by crediting each system with some crudely calculated "salvage value" instead of simply ignoring them.

The Rate of Discount

Because of uncertainties about future costs and capabilities, it is not worthwhile to devote an inordinate amount of time to refining one's estimate of "the" proper discount rate. Historical studies show that projections of cost and performance of weapon systems, particularly those made at early stages of development, have often been wide of the mark. For systems analysts to put great effort into determining "the" discount rate would probably be less productive than other uses of their time.

Moreover, because of uncertainties about future budgetary constraints and hence about marginal opportunities and their yields, the discount rate that may later be appropriate is inevitably in doubt at the time choices must be made. The best estimate may simply be a rough average rate of return in the private economy, like 6 or 8 percent. This rate would include an average allowance for risk. Special degrees of risk associated with particular weapon systems should be pointed out by the analyst but would have to be allowed for subjectively by the final decision-makers.

Indeed, for certain classes of problems, we can make a stronger case for using an average rate of return from the private economy. At the time many weapon systems are being compared, future budgetary constraints have not been set, and we can reasonably argue that the relevant options are to buy the weapons or to leave the resources in the private economy. This choice being open, the marginal opportunity is simply investment in the private economy. Hence the rate of discount that reflects what could otherwise be earned by the resources is the rate of return that could be obtained in private investment.

We can also assume, with some justification, that this rate is consistent with time preferences in the economy—with the rate of return in consumption, so to speak. That is, we can assume that future budgets fixed by the government will be consistent with time preferences as reflected by interest rates in the private sector. Individually we do not have the opportunity to adjust government outlays so that another dollar spent on government activities is as important as another dollar saved for future consumption. But the task of our governing officials is to act for us in determining budgets, and they are able to do so in the light of prevailing interest rates. For this reason, too, we might well use an average discount rate from the private sector in analyzing long-range problems of choice.

Sensitivity and Break-Even Points

In short-range problems of choice—those in which narrower resource constraints exist—the average rate of discount from the private sector is less satisfactory, even if it is the best estimate that we can make. Also in many problems, whether long-run or short-run, the risk premium may be especially troublesome. The preferred procedure may then be to regard the discount rate as "variable" and test the results for sensitivity to the rates of discount.

This procedure also yields a "break-even rate of discount"—that is, a rate of discount that makes the two leading systems equally attractive. Below this rate, one system is preferred. Above this rate, another system is best. To show such break-even points is often a useful device, especially when uncertainties are great and judgment must play a major role in reaching final recommendations. By means of this device, the analyst or policy maker can see the range of discount rates within which one policy is clearly preferred and may be able to judge that the proper rate lies within that range.

The Stipulated Capability

In view of the uncertainties, it may appear to be more straightforward and appropriate in many problems to stipulate a desired capability over future time than to do any discounting of capabilities. Indeed in many instances it may appear to be the only feasible method of handling time paths for gains or capabilities. If the enemy threat were an increasing one, so usually would be our desired capability to counter it. The stipulated capability would presumably avoid "soft spots" if our intentions were defensive; it might point toward a maximum at some particular point of time if our intentions were to take the initiative. The general considerations which cause us to discount the future might be taken into account partly by attaching little or no weight to capabilities after some arbitrary cut-off point or horizon. Also, of course, the cost streams would still be discounted to seek the lowest-cost means of achieving the stipulated capability.

Period Costing

The most common technique for comparing the costs over time of alternative systems is to add to the initial or investment costs the costs of operating each system for some fixed period, usually four or five years. Thus, one speaks of the "four-year system cost" or "five-year system cost." An end-of-period salvage value may or may not be subtracted. This is obviously a crude approximation to discounting. In effect, the discount rate is assumed to be zero during the period, rising abruptly to 100 percent at the end. But in many problems such crude devices may be completely adequate. If we are merely interested in choosing a best or better system, we can test the sensitivity of the choice to the length of the period (lengthening the period is equivalent to reducing the discount rate). If there are no great differences in the ratio of initial to annual operating cost among the various systems being compared, choice will not in fact be sensitive to the length of the period or the discount rate. Frequently, however, such differences are important—especially where some of the systems make much more extensive use of inherited assets.

Multiple Period Costing

A variant of period costing is costing over two or more periods. This increases the flexibility of the method and makes it possible to deal with more complex problems. If we are interested in an extensive future period, over which the "stipulated capability" is increasing substantially, or new systems become available to satisfy it at later dates, or both of these complications confront us simultaneously, we *may* be able to divide the future into a conveniently small number of periods, each approximately homogenous, and aggregate stipulated capabilities and costs by periods. Of course, we still have the problem of applying appropriate discount rates to the more distant future periods *as a whole*.

Lowering One's Sights

Some of the difficulties associated with time simply cannot be resolved by any kind of quantitative economic analysis. This does not mean that quantitative economic analysis has no useful role to play in connection with such problems, but it does mean that its role is subsidiary and that it must address itself to the practical problem of finding a better alternative rather than the best.

Consider, for example, the vexing question of whether to skip a generation of weapons. Sometimes vast savings in resources are possible if one skips—but at the cost of a lessened capability during the intermediate years. If we are interested in offensive or defensive weapons, there are cases where greater numbers cannot be made available or where no degree of quantitative superiority can compensate for inferiority in crucial weapon characteristics (for example if the enemy has an effective electronic counter-measure against which existing weapons possess no counter counter-measure).

At the end of World War II, the British government took a calculated (?) risk and decided to skip a generation of bombers, concentrating its resources on the development of the then advanced V-Bombers. This enabled it to cut its military budget substantially in the early post-war years, but would have left it without a modern bomber force if another war had occurred. It justified this course of action by arguing that the probability of war was low in the immediately following years. The United States Air Force was faced with a decision in the early post-war years whether to develop air-breathing missiles (like the Navajo and Snark) or whether to skip immediately to long-range ballistic missiles (Atlas). It decided to develop the air breathers. The Russians, faced by a similar choice, apparently made the opposite decision, putting their effort into the more advanced system.

Quantitative economic analysis could not have determined an optimum in a generally acceptable way in any of these cases. It could not have predicted the probability of war in the "soft" years; or the extent to which that probability would itself be affected by the softness; or the way in which the government or nation should value enhanced risk for a few years as compared with budgetary savings. But it might have been able to facilitate choice. At the very least it could have estimated quantitatively how much our capability would have been reduced for how long, and how much money would "really" have been saved. It might have been able to do something even more useful—to show how capability might have been shored up inexpensively during any soft period. Some cheap modifications of wartime bombers, for example, might have made them an effective fighting force for an unexpected emergency. Alternatively, surplus B–29's or B–50's might have been turned over to our allies as military aid and kept operational during the soft years (in fact, some were). In the missile case, air-to-surface missiles might have been a more attractive alternative than the long-range air-breathing surface-to-surface missile. Or quantitative analysis might have demonstrated that the lack of the air-breathing missiles would have had only a marginal effect on our capability, given the improved bombing aircraft that were to be operational during the soft years. Frequently, we can demonstrate that system A is better than system B even when we cannot show that system A is optimal. At a minimum, we can produce evidence relevant to the choice between A and B. And with a little ingenuity, we can often suggest a modification of A, system A', that is demonstrably better than A.

UNDERVALUING FUTURE OUTPUTS

We conclude with a final warning about the valuation of future outputs. There is a marked tendency on the part of the military services, the government, and the Congress to undervalue future capabilities. The primary responsibility of the military services is the operation of today's forces. Perhaps significantly, they always have emergency war plans, but seldom long-range war plans. Moreover, the policy of rotating service personnel at short intervals (usually three years or less) means that officials are always trying to make a recognizable mark in the very near future—later someone else will be in their jobs and responsible. Governments, similarly, have short tenure in most democracies, and many political officials have even shorter tenure. The next election always appears much more significant than the election 12 years hence—when, in any event, no rewards will be showered by the electorate on a party responsible for prescient decisions 12 years earlier. Congress (as well as an administration) is notoriously interested only in *this year's* budget and its relation to possible tax relief. The result is that within research and development almost all the resources are used in developing weapon systems with a predicted combat capability in the relatively near future; that measures that promise significant savings over a period of years are rejected because they involve somewhat higher expenditures the following year.[8] In fact, it has for this reason been almost impossible to get approval for the purchase of high performance cargo aircraft. Here let us simply point out that this bias in past and current decisions presents opportunities for quantitative economic analysis to demonstrate large gains in efficiency. In many cases, unfortunately, they will be easier to demonstrate than to sell.

---

[8] Interesting exceptions are many water and other natural resource projects which are approved in spite of the fact that they promise rates of return as low as 2½ percent. This is the opposite error: they should be required to earn at least 6 percent. In this case local benefits and log-rolling play an important role in reversing usual attitudes.

CONCLUDING OBSERVATIONS

The purpose of this book has been to explain a *way of looking* at military problems which we and others with whom we have been associated have found fruitful in insights and productive of solutions. Essentially we regard *all* military problems as, in one of their aspects, economic problems in the efficient allocation and use of resources. We believe that this way of looking at military problems goes far toward reconciling the apparent conflict of views between the officers and officials who are responsible for defense and the officials and Congressmen whose primary interest is economy—except in determining the over-all size of the military budget, where conflict between these points of view is inevitable.

While we have strong views (or prejudices) on the substantive solutions of many of the military-economic problems which we discussed, we have tried to subordinate them in writing this book. We are concerned more with how to look at military problems and how to go about solving them than with the substantive solutions themselves—which are, in any event, dependent on current circumstances and technologies and hence ephemeral. One of our aims has been to focus attention on the new problems which have become important as a result of the revolution in military technology since the development of atomic weapons. But we have tried to avoid taking sides on current controversies regarding military strategy except where the issue is too fundamental to be evaded, like the desirability of protecting our deterrent capabilities or of making preparations for localized, limited warfare. That more of our illustrative examples have been taken from Air Force rather than from Army or Navy problems in no way reflects our views regarding the relative importance of the three Services, but is the result of historical accidents that have given us greater familiarity with Air Force problems.

The book is in no sense a text in how to do military "operations research" or "systems analysis." The treatment is nonmathematical, and problems of designing detailed models of military

163

reality have been avoided. We hope, however, that operations researchers have found here the economic concepts and analysis which are essential to their craft, and that military decision-makers have found material which will enhance their understanding of operations research and their ability to use it.

INDEX

54200